The Joy of Living
and
Dying in Peace

by

His Holiness The Dalai Lama

Edited by Donald S.Lopez, Jr.

LIBRARY OF TIBETAN WORKS AND ARCHIVES

ISBN: 81-86470-69-7

Published by the Library of Tibetan Works and Archives, Dharamsala, H.P. 176215, and printed at Indraprastha Press (CBT), Nehru House, New Delhi-110002

Contents

This volume of the Path to Enlightenment series has been translated and edited by the following team: Geshey Lobsang Jordhen, a graduate of the Institute of Buddhist Dialectics, Dharamsala, who since 1989 has been religious assistant and personal translator to His Holiness the Dalai Lama; Losang Choephel Gangchenpa, who also trained at the Institute of Buddhist Dialectics and has worked as a Buddhist translator for over a decade, first at the Library of Tibetan Works and Archives, Dharamsala, and later in Australia; and Jeremy Russell, who is editor of *Chö-Yang, the Voice of Tibetan Religion & Culture*, published by the Religious and Cultural Department of the Tibetan Government-in-Exile.

Introduction

I offer these teachings for those who do not have much time or opportunity for extensive study. I have nothing to say that has not been said before. Thus, do not read this book simply for new information or new words, but try to use what I will explain to transform your mind. It is not enough simply to have heard or read something before; you should make repeated efforts to put it to use in your spiritual practice, for only then will these teachings be of true benefit.

The Buddha himself said, "Do not commit any evil deeds; collect all virtuous qualities; completely transform your mind—that is the teaching of the Buddha." The reason we should follow his advice is that in our hearts, none of us wants suffering; we all want happiness. Suffering is the result of misguided and negative deeds, but happiness is the result of positive actions. However, eliminating negativity and cultivating positive activities is not possible merely by changing our physical or verbal behavior. It can be done only by transforming the mind.

In our lives, the intelligent way of doing things is to set goals and then determine whether these goals are feasible. In the practice of Buddhism, our goal is to attain nirvana and the state of Buddhahood. As human beings we are fortunate to have the ability to achieve these goals. The state of enlightenment that we seek is freedom from the burden of disturbing emotions. The intrinsic nature of the mind is pure; the disturbing emotions that afflict it are only temporary flaws. However, we cannot eliminate negative emotions by removing certain brain cells. Even the most advanced surgical technology cannot perform this task. It can be achieved only by a transformation of the mind.

Buddhism teaches that the mind is the main cause of our being reborn in the cycle of existence. But the mind is also the main factor that allows us to gain freedom from this cycle of birth and death. This liberation is achieved by controlling negative thoughts and emotions and by promoting and developing those that are positive. It is important to realize that this task entails years of perseverance and hard work. We cannot expect instant results. Think of all the great adepts of the past. They willingly faced tremendous hardship in their quest for spiritual realization. The story of Buddha Shakyamuni is one of the best examples of this.

Motivated by compassion for all sentient beings, Buddha Shakyamuni was born more than twenty-five hundred years ago in India. He took birth as a prince. Even as a child he was mature in terms of both his knowledge and his compassion. He saw that by nature we all want happiness and do not want suffering. Suffering is not something that always comes from the outside. It does not only involve problems like famine and drought. If these were the case we could protect ourselves from suffering, for example, by storing food. But sufferings like sickness, aging, and death are problems related to the very nature of our existence, and we cannot overcome them by external conditions. What is more, we have within us this untamed mind, susceptible to all kinds of problems. It is afflicted with negative thoughts like doubt and anger. As long as our minds are beset by this host of negative thoughts, even if we have soft, comfortable clothes and delicious food to eat, they will not solve our problems.

Buddha Shakyamuni observed all these problems, and he reflected on the nature of his own existence. He found that all human beings undergo suffering, and he saw that we experience this unhappiness because of our undisciplined state of mind. He saw that our minds are so wild that often we cannot even sleep at night. Faced with this host of sufferings and problems, he was wise enough to ask whether there is a method to overcome these problems.

He decided that living the life of a prince in a palace was not the way to eliminate suffering. If anything, it was a hindrance. So he gave up all the comforts of the palace, including the companionship of his wife and son, and embarked on the homeless life. In the course of his search he consulted many teachers and listened to their instructions. He found that their teachings were of some use, but they did not provide an ultimate solution to the problem of how to eliminate suffering. He undertook six years of strict asceticism. By giving up all the facilities that he had enjoyed as a prince and engaging in strict ascetic practice, he was able to strengthen his meditative understanding. Seated beneath the Bodhi tree, he overcame the obstructive forces and attained enlightenment. Subsequently he began to teach, to turn the wheel of doctrine, based on his own experience and realization.

When we talk about the Buddha, we are not talking about someone who was a Buddha from the beginning. He began just like us. He was an ordinary sentient being who saw the same sufferings we do: birth, old age, sickness, and death. He had various thoughts and feelings, happy feelings and feelings of pain, just as we do. But as a result of his strong and integrated spiritual practice, he was able to achieve the various levels of the spiritual path culminating in enlightenment.

We should look to him as an example. We have entered this life as free and fortunate human beings and, although we are subject to a variety of sufferings, we possess human intelligence. We have a discriminative awareness. We have encountered the Buddha's vast and profound teaching and, what is more, we have the capacity to understand it. From the time of Buddha Shakyamuni up to the present day, Buddhist practitioners have taken him and subsequent sublime teachers as their inspiration.

Even though we have been born as ordinary people, we must try to use this precious opportunity before we die to gain a secure realization of the Dharma, the teachings of the Buddha. If we can do that, we will not have to fear death. A good practitioner can die peacefully without regret because his or her human potential is fulfilled. On the other hand, if, as human beings, we are unable to leave any positive imprint on our minds and only accumulate negative activities, our human potential will have been wasted. To be responsible for the pain and destruction of humans and other sentient beings is to be more like an evil force than a human being. Therefore, make this human life worthwhile, not something destructive.

In this world, people sometimes wage war in the name of religion. This happens when we take religion to be merely a label but do not actually put its meaning into practice. Spiritual practice is something with which to discipline our unruly minds. If we let ourselves be led by negative thoughts, never making an effort to transform them, and we use the Dharma to strengthen our pride, it can become a cause of war. On the other hand, if we use spiritual practice to transform our minds, there will be no chance of its becoming a cause of conflict.

Too many people have the Dharma only on their lips. Instead of using the Dharma to destroy their own negative thoughts, they regard the Dharma as a possession and themselves as the owner. They use the Dharma to wage war and for other destructive activities. Whether we profess to be Buddhist, Hindu, Christian, Jewish, or Muslim, we should not simply be satisfied by the label. What is important is to extract the message contained in these different religious traditions and to use it to transform our undisciplined minds. In short, as Buddhists we should follow the example of Buddha Shakyamuni himself.

Sometimes when I reflect on the life of Buddha Shakyamuni, I have a sense of unease. Although Buddha Shakyamuni's teaching can be interpreted on various levels, it is evident from the historical account that Buddha Shakyamuni underwent six years of hard practice. This shows that the mind cannot be transformed merely by sleeping and relaxing and enjoying all of life's comforts. It shows us that only through working hard and undergoing hardship over a long period of time will we be able to attain enlightenment. It is not easy to attain all the spiritual levels and realizations within a short time without making any effort. Even the Buddha, the proponent of the teaching we are following, had to undergo such hardship. How, then, can we expect to attain spiritual heights and become enlightened merely by performing certain so-called practices and having a relaxing time? If we read the stories of the great spiritual teachers of the past, we find that they have attained spiritual realization through a great deal of meditation, solitude and practice. They did not take any shortcuts.

If we really take refuge in the Buddha from the depths of our heart, we are bound to look to him as an example. When it comes to making the effort and undergoing hardship, the important thing is to know how to go about it. It is not as if we will be able to attain enlightenment merely by undergoing hardship and making the effort. In the Buddhist tradition, we need faith and devotion, but they must be coupled with intelligence and wisdom. Of course, we may be able to achieve a certain spiritual development through devotion and faith, but to attain nirvana and enlightenment will require wisdom as well.

In order to cultivate those positive qualities that we do not now have and to strengthen and develop those that we have already cultivated, it is important to understand the various levels of wisdom. It is important to be able to focus our intelligence and wisdom on the right subject. If a person with great intelligence is deprived of the opportunity, he or she will not be able to focus his or her intelligence on the right topic. In order to develop wisdom, we need to find the opportunity to apply our intelligence to a suitable aspect of the teaching. Therefore, Buddha Shakyamuni did not ask us simply to have faith in him. He did not solve all our problems by saying, "Have faith in me." He started by teaching the Four Noble Truths, on the basis of which he gave various levels of teaching, laying out the stages of the path to be followed.

Even the collection of the Buddha's words that were translated into Tibetan fills more than 108 volumes, which illustrates how extensively he taught. Besides these there were many teachings of the Buddha that were not translated into Tibetan. Authentic faith and wisdom are the fruit of proper study. We should try to understand and practice these teachings, which will help us develop our wisdom, assisted by the practice of compassion. Gradually we will be able to discipline our minds. In Buddhist philosophy we do not believe that things are created or motivated by some external factor. Nor do we believe that things arise from permanent causes. We relate the experiences of happiness and suffering and their causes to our own actions. And the quality of our action depends on the state of our mind—whether it is disciplined or undisciplined.

Problems and suffering arise because of an undisciplined state of mind. Therefore, our own happiness is in fact in our own hands. The responsibility rests on our own shoulders; we cannot expect someone to simply bring us happiness. The way to experience happiness is to identify its causes and cultivate them, and to identify the causes of suffering and eliminate them. If we know what is to be practiced and what is to be given up, we will naturally meet with joy.

The root of suffering is ignorance, which here means the misconception of self. All the myriad sufferings we encounter arise because of this misconception, this wrong understanding. Therefore, when it is said that the Buddha discarded all wrong views out of compassion, it means that he had the compassion to work for the benefit of all sentient beings. In order to benefit sentient beings he gave various levels of teachings that are free from wrong views and negative thoughts. Therefore, those who follow these teachings, by understanding the right view and putting it into practice, will be able to eliminate suffering. We pay homage to Buddha Shakyamuni because he gave such sublime teachings.

The Buddha is a reliable object of refuge because he initially developed compassion and then spent his whole life generating, cultivating, and nurturing compassion. In ordinary life too, whether a particular person is trustworthy or not depends upon whether he or she possesses compassion. If someone lacks compassion, we are unlikely to rely on them, even if they are intelligent and highly educated. Education alone is not enough; the basic quality that makes people helpful to other sentient beings is compassion. If someone possesses compassion or displays a mind wishing to benefit other sentient beings, we can confidently entrust ourselves to them. The most important quality of the Buddha is the mind wishing to benefit other sentient beings—compassion. Because he developed those positive qualities in himself, he has the power and the capacity to explain their importance. We can entrust ourselves to such a teacher because he has experience of these qualities.

Buddha Shakyamuni, the propounder of Buddhism, is a valid person, an infallible person, on whom we can safely rely. Still, it is not enough that he is infallible; we should know how to follow his example. We need to know how to discard the wrong path and how to cultivate and follow positive paths. Even without direct experience of these teachings, if we simply have some understanding of these things, we are in a better position to face sufferings and problems when we encounter them.

We can imagine that when two individuals encounter the same problem, depending on whether they have an understanding of the spiritual path or not, their attitudes and manners of coping with the situation will be completely different. Instead of alleviating sufferings and problems, the person with no spiritual understanding is likely to make them worse through anger, jealousy, and so forth. The person with some spiritual insight and understanding, because of his or her mental attitude, will be able to respond more openly and candidly to the situation. With some understandings of the teachings of the Buddha as well as some experience of these teachings, although we may not be able to stop suffering, we will be in a better position to deal with our problems. Therefore, we will actually derive benefit from the teachings in our daily lives.

The realms of the cycle of existence are impermanent like autumn clouds. The coming and going of sentient beings can be understood as scenes in a drama. The way sentient beings are born and die is similar to the way characters come on and off stage. Because of this impermanence, we have no lasting security. Today, we are fortunate to live as human beings. Compared to animals and those living in hell, human life is very precious. But even though we regard it as precious, life finally concludes with death. Reflecting on the whole process of human existence from beginning to end, we find that there is no lasting happiness and no security.

Even our birth is accompanied by suffering. After that, we are faced with such problems as sickness, aging, not getting what we want, and encountering situations we do not want. Some of the problems we face, like war, may be man-made. But as long as we are born in the cycle of existence and as long as disturbing emotions reside like poison in our minds, we will find no lasting peace or happiness. All the parts of a poisonous tree—its fruit, flowers, roots, leaves, and branches— will naturally be imbued with poison. Since our very existence comes under the sway of disturbing emotions, sooner or later we are bound to encounter suffering and problems as a result. Because the sufferings of sickness and death are of the nature of the cycle of existence, there is no need for surprise when we fall sick and die. Therefore, if we dislike sickness and death, we should put an end to the cycle of existence. We should put a stop to being born here again. As long as the three principal disturbing emotions of desire, hatred, and ignorance abide within us, we will constantly encounter an unsatisfactory stream of experiences. When disturbing emotions arise within our minds, they leave us without peace. So the crucial question is, how can we remove them?

Disturbing emotions are not of the same nature as the mind. If they were, then whenever the mind is present, the disturbing emotions should be present as well. But this is not the case. For example, a person may generally be very hot-tempered, but does that person remain hot-tempered and angry the entire day? Even bad-tempered people sometimes smile and relax. Therefore, even strong, disturbing emotions are not inseparable from the mind. Basically the two are separate.

Disturbing emotions are dependent on ignorance. Just as the sense of touch pervades our whole physical body, ignorance pervades all the disturbing emotions. There is no disturbing emotion that is not related to ignorance. Therefore, we must investigate what this ignorance is. Ignorance is the very powerful negative state of mind that includes all disturbing emotions. It is ignorance that casts us into the cycle of existence. But even though ignorance or the misconception of self is very strong, it is a wrong or mistaken consciousness. There are other positive minds or consciousnesses that can act as a counterforce to this ignorance. If we rely on them, we can eradicate ignorance. The nature of the mind is just clarity and awareness. In our basic nature there are no disturbing emotions; disturbing emotions are temporary obstructions of the mind. Therefore, the disturbing emotions can be removed from the basic nature of the mind. One day the mind will be enlightened, because its nature is clarity and awareness.

Right now you may not have any personal experience to lend conviction to these realities. But if you study and apply logic and analysis, you will gradually gain conviction about the possibility of removing the mind's obstructions. Generally speaking, there is a state free from disturbing emotions, called nirvana, and we can achieve that state within our own minds. Since we do not want suffering and it is possible to put an end to it and attain nirvana, there is a purpose to meditating on suffering. If we understand the whole cycle of existence as having the nature of suffering, we will engage in the practice of the three trainings—ethics, meditation, and wisdom. Then, no matter how beautiful things appear to be, we will understand that they too have the nature of suffering.

In order to cultivate an aspiration to attain nirvana, we should have some aspiration to attain a better state of life in the future. Before we do that we must appreciate the importance of this present life. If we have no understanding of the usefulness of this present life, nor of how to lead a good life by cultivating compassion and loving-kindness, there may be no purpose in discussing the possibility of attaining higher qualities in future lives. Since it is possible to become liberated from the cycle of existence, training the mind to aspire to Buddhahood is essential. We can cultivate such a motivation by reflecting that all sentient beings are like ourselves in wanting happiness and not wanting suffering. Therefore, we can each make a commitment to lead an infinite number of sentient beings to attain the unsurpassable supreme state of Buddhahood. To that end we need to become familiar with the path that leads to Buddhahood, involving practice of the twin qualities of method and wisdom.

The scriptures say that the Buddha, Dharma, and Spiritual Community are the objects of refuge for those desiring liberation. Generally speaking, there are many ways in which we seek refuge. When we are scorched by the heat of the sun, we take refuge in the shade of a tree. When we are hungry, we take refuge in food. Similarly, in hope of temporary benefit or reward, we take refuge in local gods and spirits. We find different ways of taking refuge in all the different religious traditions. For Buddhists, nirvana or the true state of cessation of suffering is the actual refuge.

What is this nirvana, this state of peace? Even though we do not want suffering, we experience it because our minds are overpowered by disturbing emotions, and because of this undisciplined state of mind we accumulate negative deeds. Therefore, the undisciplined state of our minds is the cause of suffering. If we can eliminate the causes that give rise to disturbing emotions, we will attain the state of cessation of suffering that is called nirvana or liberation, a state of true or lasting happiness. This is how the Dharma is our actual refuge.

To attain the state of the true cessation of suffering, we must follow the true path. This involves cultivating positive qualities within us. We start with the recognition that our minds are subject to ignorance, confusion, and misconception. As our understanding of the true nature of phenomena increases, we will first begin to doubt whether things have intrinsic existence. We will come to understand that objects to which we are attached, which we previously considered to be entirely good, do not have any intrinsic or substantial existence. Similarly, things that make us angry also do not have intrinsic or independent existence. By familiarizing ourselves with this understanding we will deepen our realization. Eventually we will be able to cultivate the wisdom that realizes emptiness, the true nature of phenomena, directly. This is like lighting a lamp in the darkness. This does not mean, however, that we can enlighten our minds suddenly, dispelling the darkness of ignorance much as we would turn on an electric light; cultivation of internal mental qualities must take place gradually.

Other religious traditions possess many good instructions for cultivating love and compassion, but no other religious tradition explains that things lack intrinsic existence and that everything is dependent on something else. Only the Buddhist tradition explains a state of liberation that is achieved by realizing emptiness, the real nature of all phenomena. Therefore, only the Buddha, Dharma, and Spiritual Community, or the Three Jewels, are the infallible objects of refuge for those desiring liberation or nirvana. This is what the compassionate Buddha Shakyamuni has taught.

The way we take refuge in the Three Jewels should be like that of someone in a desperate situation with nowhere else to turn. There are different kinds of faith. One is pure or clear faith, by which you appreciate the qualities of Buddha, Dharma, and Spiritual Community. Then there is the faith that is a form of trust. Next is aspiring faith.

This is more important, because in this type of faith we do not simply appreciate the qualities of the Buddha, Dharma, and Spiritual Community, but we make an effort ourselves to attain Buddhahood and to attain the qualities of the Dharma and become members of the Spiritual Community. If you are able to make such an effort, you can be sure of attaining a well-placed rebirth in your future life. If you practice sincerely in your daily life, when you come to die, you need have no regrets. What is important at the time of your death is that you be able to maintain a virtuous attitude and a pure and positive motivation. You will be able to do that because of your practice during your life. Even if you did not have much time to engage in spiritual activity during your life, if you remain alert at the time of your death and try to turn your mind toward virtuous qualities, that will definitely help you attain a well-placed rebirth.

Studying the stages of the path to enlightenment and the teachings they contain is very useful for our minds. When we study, we get the feeling that we should make a serious effort in accordance with the teachings. We feel that if we make such an effort, we will definitely be able to make spiritual progress. We may even be able to attain enlightenment. Therefore, you should not think that you are not intelligent enough, that you cannot study such teachings. If you discourage yourself you will never have another opportunity to study such instructions. All sentient beings, even the tiniest insects, are said to possess Buddha nature. Having been born as human beings we have the opportunity and capacity to understand the teaching of the Buddha.

While you listen to or read these teachings, try to relate them to your mind. Try to discover you mind's defective states and make a determination to improve them by cultivating positive qualities. If you cannot recognize your own faults, you will be unable to make any improvement. It is the general way of people that unless they pay special attention, they are not able to understand their own faults. This is why we normally claim that we have done nothing wrong. So it is extremely important to check yourself. One of our abiding habits is to continue our daily life without paying much attention to what we are doing.

Therefore it is extremely important to attend to this teaching in such a way that it contributes to the enhancement of your mind. I do not have much experience, but based on the little I do have, I can confidently assure you that you can make such progress if you try.

We have found this precious life as a free and fortunate human being, but it is not going to last forever. Sooner or later we have to face death. If we then fall into an unfavorable state of existence, it will be very difficult to find an opportunity to engage in the practice of the Dharma. We will be continually afflicted by different levels of suffering. So it is extremely important to engage in spiritual practice right now in order to keep up the momentum of cultivating virtuous qualities and eliminating the negative now and in the future. In doing so we will also gain some realization and understanding of the true path and the true cessation of suffering. Once we understand those well, we will appreciate how the Buddha is a valid and reliable teacher. We will also understand his teachings better.

It is not enough to be born in favorable states of existence as a human being or a god. As long as we do not tame and eliminate the disturbing emotions in our minds, we will find no occasion to experience joy and lasting peace. Once we acquire some understanding of what is meant by the true path and true cessation of suffering, we will be able to understand that there are powerful counterforces to the disturbing emotions and that their cessation is possible. At that point we may cultivate a strong aspiration to attain nirvana, the cessation of our personal suffering. But that too is not enough. We must proceed further to cultivate a mind wishing to attain Buddhahood for the sake of all sentient beings, to free all beings from suffering.

I have tried to explain these teachings on the basis of my own experience, which I feel may be most effective for your own minds. As spiritual practitioners we should be farsighted. Starting with a firm foundation, we should build something of spiritual value. Of course, it will take some time, but if we are farsighted to begin with and we keep up a steady effort, gradually we will be able to construct something worthwhile. Even though the goal of Buddhahood may seem far away, when it comes to our daily practice we should begin at the beginning and build on that foundation. Eventually we will reach enlightenment. And in order to practice we must know what to do and how to do it. This is why we read and listen to teachings like these.

Chapter 1

The Awakening Mind

Buddhism places great importance on inner investigation, on training to develop the mind. From a Buddhist point of view, teaching and studying the Dharma is not merely an academic pursuit. We study and teach the Dharma in order to discipline our unruly minds. In this way we can awaken our Buddha nature. We have the potential to remove those factors that obstruct our minds and gain the extraordinary powers that arise as a result.

I am happy to know that people are taking an interest in the teachings of the Buddha without necessarily being Buddhists themselves. The diverse philosophical presentations of our various religious traditions are intended to suit the diverse mental dispositions and needs we find among people. All these diverse methods and forms of practice share a common aim of helping people to become good human beings and lead a better life. Therefore, harmony among the different religious traditions is of utmost importance. And in order to achieve it we must come to understand one another's situations more clearly.

Because this is a Buddhist teaching, at the beginning we recite a verse, the first two lines of which concern taking refuge in the Buddha, Dharma, and Spiritual Community:

> Until I am enlightened I go for refuge
> To the Buddha, the Dharma and Spiritual Community.

Because it is a teaching of the Great Vehicle, the Mahayana, whereby all beings can attain freedom from suffering, the last two lines refer to cultivating the awakening mind:

By the virtue of reading or listening to this teaching,
For the sake of all wandering beings, may I attain the state
of a Buddha.

The awakening mind is the intention to achieve Buddhahood
in order to free all beings in the universe from suffering. In order to
develop the awakening mind, we must meditate; it cannot be
cultivated merely by wishful thinking and prayers. It cannot be
cultivated merely by gaining an intellectual understanding of what
it means. Nor can it be cultivated simply by receiving blessings. We
have to cultivate it through meditation and repeated and prolonged
habituation. In order to be able to sustain meditation on the
awakening mind, we need first to appreciate the benefits of its
cultivation. We need to develop an intense longing to cultivate the
awakening mind, seeing it as a pressing need.

If we take delight in the practice, our meditation is more likely
to succeed. The noble mind wishing to benefit others is extremely
fruitful. It is the principal source of happiness, courage, and success
in life. When our minds are full of suspicion and ill will, we
automatically feel that others think badly of us. These negative feelings
color all our relations with our fellow human beings. More often
than not they lead to unhappiness. This is natural. Therefore, even
in the terms of this life, the more altruistic we are, the happier we
will be. The more we are affected by ill will and hatred, the unhappier
we will be.

Whether we seek happiness for ourselves or for others and
whether we seek temporary or long-term happiness, we need this
noble mind of compassion even in this life. Similarly, if we wish to
achieve a well-placed rebirth as a human or celestial being over
successive lives in the future, we must cultivate a good heart. Higher
rebirth is a result of practices such as not taking the lives of other
beings. In fact, higher rebirth is due to giving up all acts that harm
the body, life, possessions, friends, and relations of others, and to
practicing the ten virtuous actions (sustaining life, giving gifts,
maintaining sexual ethics, speaking truthfully, speaking
harmoniously, speaking kindly, speaking sensibly, generosity, helpful

intent, and right view.) We accumulate the positive causes leading to the attainment of such rebirth by stopping activities that harm others. The root of such practices is a good-hearted attitude toward others.

When we consult a doctor, most of us are told to rest. But what does it mean to rest? It means more than simply lying in bed. Rest means remaining mentally relaxed. Whether the doctor is able to spell it out to us or not, when he advises us to rest, he means that we should be mentally relaxed and free from anxiety, in addition to avoiding physical activity. Then we will get real rest. Mental relaxation is the result of having a positive mental attitude and feelings. If our minds are invaded by negative attitudes and we brood on ill will, mental relaxation is impossible. Therefore, even in relation to our physical health, when we are told to rest, there is a sense in which we are being advised to "be a warm-hearted person," because this is the best way to avoid anxiety.

It is for reasons such as these that whenever the great Indian saint and scholar Atisha met anyone he would ask, "Do you have a good mind?" in the same way that we nowadays say, "How are you?" He was not really asking whether the person he was talking to was warm-hearted, but how he or she was, how he or she had been faring that day. But his way of asking the question has a deeper meaning. I do not think Atisha addressed people in this way merely from a religious point of view. He was asking, "Are you well rested?" in the way we might ask, "Did you sleep well?" because rest is the fruit of a positive mind.

It is thus obvious that it is worthwhile to cultivate a good heart, but the question is how to go about it. When it comes to training the mind, a good heart refers to the awakening mind, which is the best, supreme, and ultimate mode of the good heart. It is an unlimited good mind complemented by wisdom. The scriptures explain that the awakening mind is a mind with two aspirations. It is a mental consciousness induced by (1) an aspiration to fulfill the purposes of others, assisted by (2) an aspiration to achieve Buddhahood.

Now, what do we mean when we say "complemented by wisdom"? Let us take the case of a mind taking refuge in the Buddha. Such a state of mind might involve accepting that the Buddha is an ultimate object of refuge free from all faults and possessing all qualities. It could simply be accepting that the Buddha is a precious and holy being. It could be a matter of faith. But there is also another process of taking refuge based on analysis and inquiry regarding the nature of such a Buddha and the possibility of his or her existence. As a result of such an examination, we can come to understand that such a Buddha is possible. We come to understand the nature of the Buddha, that he or she possesses a mind with unique qualities, free from all obstructions. And having understood the meaning of such a superior Buddha we can cultivate a deep sense of taking refuge in the Buddha based on conviction. This is much stronger and more stable than mere faith.

Cultivating the awakening mind is similar to this. It is possible for there to be a bodhisattva who has not understood emptiness yet but at the same time has a wholehearted aspiration to fulfill the purposes and wishes of sentient beings. Based on that aspiration he or she could generate a mind aspiring to Buddhahood for the sake of all sentient beings. But usually when we talk about the awakening mind, it is based on investigating whether the sufferings of infinite sentient beings can be eliminated and, if so, determining the means for doing so. Based on such reflections and thoughts we examine the meaning of enlightenment, as stated in the following lines:

Compassion focusing on sentient beings
And wisdom focusing on enlightenment.

When we cultivate the noble awakening mind wishing to achieve enlightenment for the sake of sentient beings augmented by the knowledge that enlightenment can be achieved, it becomes a wonderful and courageous mind.

It also makes a great difference when compassion is supported by the wisdom realizing the emptiness of intrinsic existence. In general, by focusing on one helpless sentient being, we generate a strong wish that he or she be free from suffering because we are unable to bear his or her suffering. But if we analyze more deeply, we will be able to see where that suffering comes from. We will understand the possibility of removing its causes and the possibility of cultivating antidotes within that person. We will be able to see all these possibilities within that person, but also that he or she is really confused about the way things exist and does not know how to cultivate such positive antidotes. We can see not only that the person is currently encountering suffering, but moreover that he or she engages in many negative activities. He or she is dominated by faults that will lead to the experience of unceasing suffering in the future.

Clearly seeing the possibility of eliminating suffering, but also knowing that out of ignorance sentient beings still do not know how to implement ways to free themselves from suffering, we cultivate a very powerful sense of concern and compassion. It is like seeing a person who could have easily solved a problem but does not do so, either because of ignorance of the ways and means or because of lack of initiative. When we observe a sentient being afflicted with suffering we should know that he or she is just like us and does not want suffering. We cultivate a wishful thought: "How good it would be if this suffering could be eliminated; may this suffering come to an end." If we also understand the ways and means leading to the state of freedom from suffering and see others' suffering in the light of that knowledge, our compassion is much more powerful.

When we train in the awakening mind we should train in these two aspirations: the aspiration toward Buddhahood and the aspiration wishing to benefit others. The source of the aspiration to benefit others, the awakening mind that has greater concern for others than oneself, is compassion. In the course of cultivating genuine compassion, we train in the mind that has strong concern for sentient beings afflicted by suffering and in the mind that views suffering sentient beings as pleasing and lovable. But at the same time we should be able to see the nature of the sufferings by which these sentient beings are afflicted. We should train in these two separately.

In order to clearly identify suffering it is important first to think about the suffering we experience ourselves. It is much easier to identify suffering in this way. Therefore, we often say that the mind of compassion and the determination to be free from the sufferings of the cycle of existence are like two sides of the same coin. Reflecting upon the suffering in our own lives and training our minds to get rid of it is the determination to be free. When we apply the same wish to overcome suffering to other sentient beings, we cultivate compassion.

The foundation for reflecting upon our own sufferings and gaining the determination to be free from them is the teaching of the Four Noble Truths. This is the most crucial of all the Buddha's teachings. The Four Noble Truths can be classified into two categories. The first two truths, true sufferings and true origins, are the set of distressing causes and effects associated with the disturbing emotions and the sufferings that we want to overcome. The second set of two, true cessations and true paths, are the set of causes and effects of the pure category. Having reflected upon suffering we might wonder what we can do about it. The last two noble truths reveal a complete path for our future course of action. If this path had not been taught or if such a path could not be followed, we would be merely punishing ourselves by reflecting upon the first two noble truths of suffering and its cause. It would be better simply to relax and enjoy ourselves. What would be the point of thinking about suffering? But when we are advised to think about suffering, it is because there is a means of release from it; it is proper to reflect upon suffering, because such reflection stimulates our determination to be free. This is why the teaching of the Four Noble Truths is so crucial and important.

To help our meditation, there are three principal ways to think about suffering. These are the suffering of pain, the suffering of change, and the pervasive suffering that is a condition of existence. The suffering of pain refers to the common distress and trouble that we ordinarily identify as suffering. The suffering of change refers to the flawed happiness that we usually aspire to. The reason such happiness is flawed is that it does not last, it finally comes to an end. Because such experiences of happiness eventually change into suffering, they are called the suffering of change. The basis of all these experiences is this physical body, which is subject to karma and disturbing emotions. These provide the conditions for this involuntary and unceasing continuity of physical rebirth. We experience unending suffering because it is a condition of existence, and therefore it is called the pervasive suffering of conditioning.

Each of the Four Noble Truths can be explained according to four attributes. The four attributes of true sufferings are impermanence, suffering, emptiness, and selflessness. The impermanence of true sufferings refers to their subtle impermanence. Whatever is produced through cause and effect is subject to momentary change and disintegration. Its disintegration is due to the very causes by which it has been produced. It does not depend on some other subsequent cause. Causes and conditions create true sufferings in such a way that by their very nature they disintegrate and change from moment to moment. Therefore, true sufferings are clearly dependant on their causes.

When we examine this collection of physical and mental components that we think of as our body and mind, we can understand that it is impermanent by nature. It changes from moment to moment. This is because it is dependant on causes, the chief of which is ignorance. Since this collection of physical and mental components is a product of ignorance, we can understand that its very nature is suffering.

By reflecting on this description of subtle impermanence we will come to understand that ignorance is the basic cause of our collection of physical and mental components. So long as we are dependent on ignorance, so long as we are the product of ignorance, no matter where we stay or what kind of birth we take, we are finally subject to destruction. Whether our physical form is attractive or ugly, large or small, it is subject to change. If we are able to understand this from the depths of our mind, we will not be discouraged by minor and immediate hardships. We will understand that so long as we are not freed from the bondage of the disturbing emotions, it is impossible to obtain real and secure happiness. This is the way to train our minds.

When we train our minds in this way, we will be able to see disturbing emotions as our real enemy. Residing peacefully at the center of our hearts from beginningless time, they have brought us only suffering and harm. Identifying these disturbing emotions as the real enemy, we can start to fight them to the best of our ability. As the Kadampa masters, the great Tibetan practitioners of the twelfth and thirteenth centuries, used to say: "Even if we are completely overpowered and weighed down by our enemy, this heavy load of disturbing emotions, the only thing to do is to grit our teeth. Do not accept defeat."

On the other hand, we should cultivate a mind that wholeheartedly detests disturbing emotions. On the other, we should understand that so long as we are overwhelmed by ignorance, it will be impossible to find genuine happiness. The question is whether ignorance can be eliminated or not. This is made clear by the third noble truth, true cessation of suffering. The Buddha explained this third truth in great detail. The fact that all beings have the Buddha nature has two important implications. The first is that the faults or defilements of the mind are adventitious, and the second is that the qualities of a Buddha can be achieved. When we examine and think about these two points, we can infer the possibility of achieving the true cessation of suffering. This is how we cultivate a genuine wish for nirvana or liberation.

If we find such faults in this cycle of existence, are there any alternative ways of living? Once we become aware of the existence of nirvana, a mind wishing to achieve it arises. Disturbing emotions are the chief obstacle to our achieving liberation. Therefore, we come to view disturbing emotions as our enemy, and a desire arises to combat and defeat this enemy. When it comes to actual practice, it is difficult initially to fight and put a stop to this enemy. Because the chief cause of disturbing emotions is ignorance, when we talk about putting a stop to disturbing emotions, we have to put a stop to ignorance. The only factor that can really do that is the wisdom understanding selflessness. In order to cultivate the wisdom realizing selflessness, it is not enough just to understand what it means. It is not enough to have occasional thoughts about the meaning of selflessness. We have to meditate on the meaning of selflessness or emptiness single-mindedly. Only if we gain real insight will we be able gradually to eliminate the various levels of disturbing emotions. In short, it is necessary to meditate on and familiarize ourselves with the view of selflessness for a long time.

To cultivate this special insight into selflessness, we need the support of the practice of meditative stabilization. The foundation of such a practice is restraint from negative conduct. Until we are in a position actually to go on the offensive against our disturbing emotions, we should first adopt the defensive stance of controlling our negative behavior. Our random accumulation of misdeeds is the result of being dominated by disturbing emotions.

Our principal misdeeds committed under the sway of disturbing emotions are summarized as the ten unwholesome actions. Physically these are killing, stealing, and sexual misconduct. Verbally they include lying, divisive talk, harsh speech, and idle gossip. And mentally they consist of covetousness, harmful intention, and wrong view. When we are at risk of engaging in any of these ten actions, we should apply antidotes and restrain ourselves from them. Refraining from the ten unwholesome actions is the practice of the ten virtues. For this we need to be convinced of the validity of the principle of cause and effect, the law of karma. If we accumulate causes harmful in nature, we will experience suffering when the causes come to fruition. If we engage in acts that are beneficial by nature, we will experience peace and happiness as a result. The stronger our conviction that good results arise from good causes and bad results arise from bad causes, the more easily will we adopt good practices and give up negative ways of life.

The birth that we have obtained in this life has unique potential. Human beings are the same as other sentient beings in possessing life, but far excel other beings in their ingenuity and intelligence. If we acknowledge the opportunity provided by human life as something precious and worthwhile, we will be able to use our human intelligence in the right way. For example, when we understand their negative consequences, we are able to see why the ten unwholesome actions are faulty. As a result of engaging in these ten unwholesome actions we will be projected into miserable states of existence, for example, as animals. To appreciate the sufferings of such states of existence we can observe the lives of animals that are visible to us. Since we do not want to experience such sufferings ourselves, we can avoid them by realizing that they are the result of negative deeds. When we train our minds gradually in this way, we will be able to identify suffering and cultivate a determination to be free of it.

Once we have a clear understanding of the sufferings with which we are afflicted, we should change the object and reflect in a similar way upon the sufferings of other sentient beings. Then we should train our minds in aspiring to benefit other sentient beings. Suffering sentient beings are not unrelated to us; our own future happiness and suffering are very much dependent on them. The cultivation of the noble mind wishing to benefit others is a marvelous thing. Even when we are trying to pursue our own interests, the more we cultivate a mind wishing to benefit others, the more quickly our own purposes will be fulfilled. Thus there is great benefit in cultivating such a mind. The first thing to understand is that other beings are not somehow separate from and unrelated to us.

We should train our mind systematically to see all sentient beings as pleasing and close to us. To begin this training, we should meditate on mental equanimity. Normally we feel close to those who benefit us, referring to them as our friends or relatives. Those with whom we are currently not on good terms we refer to as our enemies, and we have a feeling of distance from them. For example, when we Tibetans hear about sufferings and tragedies that take place in Tibet, we gather together in the temple to say prayers. But when we hear about a flood in China, instead of praying for the victims, we might rejoice. This is a clear indication of the partiality of our spiritual practice. The practice of equanimity is aimed at correcting this unbalanced attitude. People who are currently our friends have not necessarily been our constant friends in all our past lives. They have at times been our enemies. People whom we currently regard as enemies have not always been so throughout our many past lives. They have been our friends as well. There is no sound reason for maintaining partiality. Even in this life, as the great master Gungthang has said, our so-called best friend becomes our sworn enemy because of one wrong word. Those who were our friends in the early part of our lives may become our enemies later on, and vice versa. This is evident to all of us. This kind of attitude of partiality must be eliminated, because it is based on attachment and anger. A clear sign of this is that as soon as the other person's behavior changes, we also change our behavior. On the other hand, if we had a genuine feeling of closeness toward other sentient beings that took account of their situation, even if other people's attitudes changed, ours would remain the same. When we talk about someone who is a friend or relative, we always say, "*my* friend, *my* relative." We emphasize our relationship because of attachment. This is the kind of partiality we have to guard against. As long as we have such feelings of partiality, we will not be able to see the sameness of all other sentient beings. For that reason we should reflect that even our best friend might have been our enemy in a past life. Once we are able to cultivate a feeling of the equality of all sentient beings, we will be able to appreciate their kindness.

Therefore, our sworn enemy should be the disturbing emotions, not our fellow beings who are also overpowered and afflicted by disturbing emotions. In cultivating compassion, it is important first to thoroughly understand what we mean by different levels of sufferings. Usually when we see people who are afflicted with some physical suffering or who are handicapped, we immediately feel compassion for them. But when we see people who are wealthy or well educated, instead of generating compassing we feel jealous and want to compete with them. This clearly indicates that our compassion is partial and lopsided, because we are not aware of the sufferings that pervade the minds of all sentient beings. Therefore, it is extremely important to recognize the disturbing emotions residing within us as the real enemy. Once we understand that, we will be able to understand the problems that arise in the minds of other sentient beings because of the disturbing emotions. Compassion should be cultivated toward all sentient beings. To identify a particular group of sentient beings as friends or relatives and maintain a special feeling of closeness toward them is actually attachment, not genuine compassion. And the result of obsessive attachment is suffering. Therefore, we should cultivate a sense of equanimity toward others, free of feelings of partiality, attachment, and hatred.

The next step is to see all sentient beings as our relatives. There is hardly a single sentient being who has not been one of our relatives, such as our mother, in the past. In the future too they will definitely become our friends and relatives again. From this perspective we should try to remember their kindness when, for example, they were our mothers. Then we should think about how to repay their kindness. After that, we should then cultivate equanimity again, focusing here on the equality of ourselves and others. All sentient beings, regardless of their backgrounds, are the same as us in wanting happiness and not wanting suffering. Therefore, we train our minds to think that since other sentient beings are like ourselves, it is not appropriate to differentiate between them, generating hatred toward one group and attachment toward another.

A special way of remembering the kindness of others is to reflect that sentient beings have been kind and beneficial to us not only because they have been our relatives, but also in many other ways, direct and indirect. Let us think about the present state of human existence. We are all closely interlinked. Whatever we enjoy is the result of other people's work. Manufactured goods are assembled by people working in factories. The raw materials used in their production are mined from the earth by other people. All the facilities and comforts we enjoy while we read or listen to this teaching are the work of countless sentient beings. We can enjoy ourselves due to their hardship. Likewise we are able to cultivate the precious awakening mind only because there are countless helpless sentient beings without a guide. It is because of the kindness of friendly sentient beings that we are able to cultivate the awakening mind. Even the ultimate attainment of the state of Buddhahood is possible only because of the kindness of sentient beings. Not only are we the same as all other sentient beings, but sentient beings are very kind to us. Therefore, by recalling their kindness we are able to see sentient beings as attractive and close to us. We can understand how sentient beings have been kind in the beginning, middle, and end.

Having considered the kindness of other beings, we also have to reflect on the faults of our own self-centered attitude and the benefits of being more concerned for the welfare of others. When we appreciate the disadvantages and advantages of these two opposing attitudes, we will be able to cultivate a mind wishing to exchange ourselves with others. Until now we have regarded ourselves as very precious. Now we transfer this concern to other sentient beings and regard them as very precious. Until now we have simply neglected other sentient beings. Now we recognize that compared to the more important cause of fulfilling the wishes of all other sentient beings, our personal needs are insignificant. This is what is referred to as the practice of exchanging oneself with others.

When we train our minds in this way, regardless of the way other sentient beings live or behave, we will be able to cultivate a mind seeing all sentient beings as pleasing and attractive. On that basis the practices of giving and taking are taught. Giving focuses primarily on love, because giving here means to imagine giving away all your virtue and happiness to others. Taking focuses primarily on compassion, because taking here means to imagine taking all of the suffering and nonvirtue of others onto yourself. By doing such practices we will be able to cultivate an especially strong sense of responsibility. This is how we train the mind to work for the benefit of others.

As explained above, when we gain conviction of the possibility of achieving nirvana within ourselves, we will appreciate that other sentient beings also have the same opportunity. On the basis of such an understanding we develop an aspiration or wish to deliver all sentient beings to the state of nirvana. Then we cultivate the realization that in order to do so, we must first achieve enlightenment ourselves—there is no other option. So we aspire to achieve enlightenment as a means of helping others and fulfilling their purposes. This requires an unshakable resolution, courage, and commitment. Such a mind is called the awakening mind.

The more we cultivate a mind wishing to benefit other sentient beings, the greater will be the peace and happiness within ourselves. If we have inner peace ourselves, we will be better able to contribute to the peace and happiness of others. Transforming our minds and cultivating a positive attitude is the very source of happiness for many lives to come. Maintaining a positive attitude gives us the opportunity to remain relaxed, to become more courageous, and to keep our spirits up. For myself, I have tried to leave some positive imprints within my mind by steadily studying the stages of the path and familiarizing myself with them. As a result, when I confront problems I find them easier to handle, because I know about the sufferings of the realms of existence. When I remember the instruction that everything is subject to destruction and sufferings are bound to come, I do not lose heart. And of course I have never thought about committing suicide. So this is a clear indication that the teaching can really help us in our lives.

I am now more than sixty years old, and I have accumulated enough experience to be able to say with confidence that the Buddha's teachings and instructions are relevant and useful. If you sincerely put the gist of these teachings into practice, there is no question about their being useful in your present life and for many lives to come. Such practices are useful for yourself and for all sentient beings. They also give us guidelines for preserving and living in harmony with the environment. It is not that these teachings were useful at some time in the past and are no longer relevant. They are extremely relevant and applicable today.

When we are advised to engage in such practices it is not simply in order that the tradition be preserved. However, the time that we spend reading and thinking about this teaching does make a great contribution to the tradition. It allows us to create something of spiritual value in our minds. When someone constructs a temple or stupa, everybody expresses their appreciation and thinks of it as Dharma practice. However, attending to the teachings is even more important, because the resultant spiritual construction will help us for many lives to come. External constructions, however well you make them, will crumble and disintegrate. What we create within our minds will last much much longer.

The most important thing initially is to prepare ourselves to make successful use of this life and to ensure that we have the opportunity and capacity to practice in future lives. Furthermore, we should understand that all disturbed and afflicted states of the mind are brought about by the internal enemy, the disturbing emotions. As long as the disturbing emotions reside within our minds and as long as we are a slave to them, we will have neither peace nor happiness. We may have many comfortable facilities at our disposal, but they are fleeting in nature and cannot guarantee lasting happiness. Thus, we should not be focused merely on our future lives, but must be concerned with getting rid of the disturbing emotions entirely. It is on the basis of this attitude that we aspire to attain nirvana or the state of liberation from the cycle of existence. If we extend our minds even further, we embark on a greater endeavor than a better rebirth or our own liberation from suffering. We think not only about ourselves but also about the welfare of all other sentient beings. This training is like a child's progress through school. Beginning with kindergarten, the child gradually acquires more education and broadens its perspective. This is the way to create something worthwhile within our minds. By cultivating such a mind we replace our present mental attitude, which is concerned only with our own welfare, with a mind more concerned with the happiness of all sentient beings.

Life as a free and fortunate human being is precious because it gives us the opportunity to cultivate the awakening mind. It provides us with the potential to achieve great things. Therefore, once we have found such an opportunity, it will be a great tragedy if we are unable to make good use of it. No other creature can challenge the human potential and capacity to create benefit. But not everyone who has attained a human life is free and fortunate. Being free and fortunate from a Buddhist perspective means being free to practice the Dharma and having access to the necessary conditions to do so. Insects and other animals, for instance, even though they possess life, do not have such freedom and fortune. People who have been born in a place where the Dharma is practiced and have at least some sense of compassion and concern for the welfare of other sentient beings are regarded as free and fortunate human beings.

There are now more than 5 billion people in this world. But how many of these either are influenced by the teaching of the Buddha or have genuine concern for their fellow human beings? Compared to the number of other creatures in the world, the number of human beings is very small. Among human beings, the number who follow some kind of religious faith is even smaller, and among those the number who are moved by genuine compassion and loving-kindness for other people is even smaller still. Such a life is very difficult to find, because the causes and conditions that give rise to it are difficult to establish.

We should never think that we do not have the capacity to do serious practice or cultivate fresh qualities. Regardless of our age or intelligence, compared to other animals, we all have a great capacity for the practice of the Dharma. Even when we are old and frail, we still have human intelligence. We should never become discouraged because we feel handicapped in some way. Young people particularly should not be despondent. We should take inspiration from the many people in the past who engaged in sincere study, practice, and meditation and achieved great realization. These saintly scholars greatly benefited themselves and others. We should follow their example.

Having found such a precious opportunity as this life as a free and fortunate human being, if we are unable to do something beneficial with it, it will be difficult to find such a human life in the future. We have a saying in Tibet that engaging in virtuous practice is as hard as pulling a tired donkey up a hill, but engaging in negative, destructive activities is as easy as rolling a boulder down a steep slope. Our tendency is to engage in negative activities even while thinking that we should not. Whether we think of ourselves as a fully ordained monk or a great tantric practitioner or simply as a Dharma practitioner, it is often the case that either our motivation is not good in the beginning, or that our actual practice of visualization and meditation is not good in the middle, or that our conclusion is not good. All of our virtuous practices are interrupted by negative thoughts, so they remain weak and frail. A flash of lightening on a dark and cloudy night allows us to see our surroundings for just a moment. Likewise, this opportunity to meet and practice the Buddha's teachings is rare and short-lived. Our virtuous qualities are weak because our motivation, actual practice, and conclusion are weak, while our negative deeds are powerful and unending. Therefore, it is important to make a special effort to cultivate fresh positive qualities.

Only the awakening mind, which leads to enlightenment, has the power to exhaust powerful negative deeds. After countless eons examining what would be most beneficial for sentient beings, Buddha Shakyamuni concluded that it was the awakening mind. The Buddhas of the past cultivated the awakening mind with a wish to relieve all suffering sentient beings. They accumulated merit for countless eons and finally became enlightened. Every one of them found from their own experience that the awakening mind is beneficial to all. This is because the awakening mind, a mind wishing to benefit all other sentient beings, is responsible for the achievement of all positive virtuous qualities. This mind wishing to benefit all other sentient beings is solely responsible for their swift attainment of peace and happiness. Whether we are concerned with the initial stage of practice, with cultivating fresh spiritual qualities, or with the attainment of Buddhahood itself, they all depend on cultivating the awakening mind. Even in ordinary life, the mind wishing to benefit other sentient beings is priceless. When we have such a positive attitude it brings happiness to ourselves and others. It enables us to plant the seed of happiness for all sentient beings and ensure harmony with the environment.

Someone who has lived a dog's life imprisoned in the cycle of existence is called a bodhisattva from the moment he or she generates the awakening mind. From that moment, such a person is worthy of the respect of human beings and gods. The awakening mind is like an elixir that can transform base iron into gold. This is because when we cultivate the awakening mind within ourselves, even our external behavior, the way we speak and the way we behave toward other people, can be transformed. Our other virtuous qualities are like the plantain tree, which produces one fruit and perishes, but the awakening mind is like a wish-fulfilling celestial tree that enables us to reap endless fruit. Relying on the awakening mind we will soon be liberated and free from suffering and fear.

The awakening mind is a mind wishing to deliver all sentient beings to the state of enlightenment. It is a mind wishing to attain enlightenment in ourselves in order to help suffering sentient beings. To develop it, we must recognize that the infinite sentient beings are of the same nature as ourselves. They want happiness and do not want suffering. Like ours, the nature of their minds is clear light. Their mental obstructions are temporary and adventitious. This is not to say that their mental obstructions do not exist. They have been there from beginningless time. But the intrinsic quality of the mind, its potential to attain the powers and qualities of the Buddha, is also present right from the start. At an ordinary level we are unable to become omniscient or enlightened because of certain obstructions and hindrances. As soon as we remove these hindrances and obstructions our minds will be aware of all phenomena.

Finding happiness and overcoming suffering are the natural rights of all sentient beings. We are all the same in having the opportunity to find happiness and to remove suffering. The difference is that personal happiness or suffering is related to just one single individual, but the suffering and happiness of other sentient beings relate to countless sentient beings. When we compare the two, the happiness of countless sentient beings takes on far greater importance than personal interest. Based on such an understanding, we will seek the causes of happiness for other sentient beings.

When we talk about delivering other sentient beings to the state of nirvana, it cannot be done by distributing wealth or even through personal miraculous power. They only way is to show them the right path to reach the state of nirvana. To do that we should first know ourselves the different stages of the path leading to nirvana. Unless we are able to show the path leading to nirvana from our own experience, our help will be limited. Therefore, we generate an aspiration to attain enlightenment for the sake of all sentient beings. The marvelous, wonderful awakening mind is called a jewel-like mind, the most precious of all minds. Merely generating the awakening mind is a source of great merit. Even within the cycle of existence it will provide great fruit, such as peace of mind and the chance to live in a harmonious environment. Nevertheless, the flow of merit becomes continuous and unceasing only after the awakening mind becomes the motivation for our deeds. Once we vow to engage in the deeds of a bodhisattva, the flow of merit will be continuous and unceasing like the limitless expanse of space.

If the mere wish to benefit other sentient beings is more effective than making offerings to the Buddhas, then trying to actually benefit infinite sentient beings is better still. If all sentient beings want happiness and do not want suffering, we might ask why we cannot let them work hard for their own happiness and to remove their own suffering. The answer is that even though sentient beings desire to remove suffering, they run continuously toward it. And even though they want happiness, because of their ignorance and confusion they continuously destroy their own peace and happiness. The awakening mind brings peace and happiness to those deprived of them. There is no virtue comparable to the awakening mind.

When we praise someone who repays another's kindness, what need be said about bodhisattvas who work for the welfare of other sentient beings without being asked? Giving a single meal sufficient to allay a person's hunger for half a day is ordinarily regarded with admiration. Then what need be said about a bodhisattva who works over limitless time to establish countless sentient beings in the unsurpassed peace of Buddhahood, thereby fulfilling all their desires? If we are able to cultivate such a mind benefiting other sentient beings, we will automatically accumulate great merit, the source of peace and happiness. Once we commit ourselves to fulfilling the purposes of other sentient beings, our own purposes will be fulfilled by the way. Therefore, I often tell people that if they want the best for themselves, they should work to benefit other people. Those people who ignore the welfare of other sentient beings and think only of themselves are trying to fulfill their wishes in a very foolish way.

When we talk about democracy or democratic rights, we are talking about caring for the welfare of the majority. The more we care for the welfare of the majority, the more we work for social welfare, the greater will be our own peace and happiness. On the other hand, if we take a dictatorial approach and try to bully our way through life and impose our views on the minds of other people, we will not be able to fulfill their desires and wishes or our own. Therefore, it is a law of nature that the more people are bullied and oppressed, the more unhappiness there will be. Equally, the more we work to benefit other people, the greater will be the benefit for all. Just as the citizens of a particular country have certain obligations as well as enjoying certain benefits, our obligation as followers of the Buddhas and bodhisattvas is to benefit all sentient beings. This is what we make a commitment to do. To reinforce it we purify all our past misdeeds by admitting them openly, and we undertake not to repeat them in the future. We commit ourselves henceforth to do what is beneficial to other sentient beings and to abstain from what harms them.

This, in sum, is the process the majority of us should pursue. Some exceptional people may find liberation quickly, because of their past karmic potential. But the majority of us cannot hope to reach enlightenment or nirvana so miraculously. When we plant a seed or a sapling, we do not expect to get fruit and flowers immediately. As a child, I remember planting some seeds. Then, without giving them time to grow, I would dig them up to see how they were doing. This is not the way. We have to let nature take its course. If we try to violate the law of nature and expect sudden enlightenment, we will be disappointed. I have jokingly suggested before that our frequent talk of attaining enlightenment within three years and three months is usually as far-fetched as Chinese propaganda. We go into retreat intent on enlightenment, but three years and three months later we come back the same ordinary person, with perhaps slightly longer hair. That is why it is important to be farsighted and to aspire to enlightenment even if we have to work for countless eons.

The awakening mind is the exclusive cause of the achievement of Buddhahood. In order to cultivate such a mind it is extremely important to purify negative deeds and accumulate merit. Once we have begun to feel the effects on our minds of cultivating the awakening mind and we have begun to appreciate it in our own experience, we should stabilize it by receiving the aspirational awakening mind in a ceremony after which one vows actually to pursue the bodhisattva's way of life.

CHAPTER 2

Dying in Peace

Something that preoccupies us all is how to live and die peacefully.
Death is a form of suffering, it is an experience we would rather
avoid, and yet it is something that will definitely befall each and every
one of us. Nevertheless, it is possible to adopt a course of action so that
we can face this unwelcome event without fear. One of the principal
factors that will help us to remain calm and undisturbed at the time of
death is the way we have lived our lives. The more we have made our
lives meaningful, the less we will regret at the time of death. The way
we feel when we come to die is thus very much dependent on the way
we have lived.

If our daily life is somehow positive and meaningful, when the end
comes, even though we do not wish for it, we will be able to accept it as
a part of our life. We will have no regrets. You might ask what we mean
by making our daily life meaningful. Our present human existence is not
aimed at brining more suffering upon ourselves and others. Human beings
are social animals and our happiness is dependent on many factors. If we
live in harmony with reality we will make our life meaningful.

We cannot live alone in isolation. We need sufficient food, clothing,
and shelter, all of which come about due to the efforts of many other
people. Our basic happiness is dependent on others. Living in
accordance with this reality is a meaningful way to spend our lives.
Since others are the objects on whom our peace and happiness depend,
it is proper for us to take care of them. But we tend instead to think
that we have achieved everything by ourselves.

We need to develop a wider perspective, even though our main
concern may be our own personal well-being. Once we develop a wider

perspective, a sense of concern for and commitment to others will automatically arise. This is not something holy or sacred. It is simply that our own future is heavily dependent on others. This kind of view is not only realistic, it is also a basis for a kind of secular ethics. Trying to solve problems using force results in a disregard for others' rights and views. A nonviolent approach is a human approach, because it involves dialogue and understanding. Human dialogue can be achieved only through mutual respect and understanding in a spirit of reconciliation. This is a way to make our daily lives meaningful.

Usually, when I describe the essence of Buddhism, I say that at best we should try to help others, and if we cannot help them at least we should do them no harm. That is the essence of the Buddha's teaching. I think this point is relevant even from a secular point of view. If an individual relates to others with compassion, in the long run he or she will definitely be a happier person. Negative activities may result in temporary gain, but deep in your heart you will always feel uneasy. A compassionate attitude does not mean a mere passive feeling of pity. In a competitive modern society sometimes we need to take a tough stand. But we can be tough and compassionate. When someone who lives in this way comes to the end of his or her life, I am certain he or she will die happily and without regret.

Embarking on a spiritual practice that is measured in lifetimes and eons gives you a different perspective on death. In the context of our existence through many successive lives, death is something like changing your clothes. When your clothes become old and worn out, you change them for new ones. This affects your attitude toward death. It gives rise to a clearer realization that death is a part of life. Grosser levels of mind are dependent on our brains, so they continue to function only as long as the brain functions. As soon as the brain stops, these levels of mind automatically stop. The brain is a condition for the appearance of grosser levels of mind, but the substantial cause of the mind is the continuity of the subtle mind, which has no beginning.

When we are dying, other people can remind us to generate positive states of mind up to the point at which the gross level of consciousness dissolves. But once we have entered the state of subtle consciousness, only the force of our previous predispositions can help. At that point it is very difficult for anyone else to remind us about virtuous practice. Therefore, it is important to develop an awareness of death and to become familiar with ways to cope with the dissolution of the mind right from the time of our youth. We can do this by rehearsing it through visualization. Then, instead of being afraid of death, we may feel a sense of excitement about it. We may feel that having made preparations for so many years, we should be able to meet the challenge of death effectively.

Once you have an experience of the deeper subtle mind in meditation, you can actually control your death. Of course, that can be done only when you reach an advanced level of practice. In tantra there are advanced practices such as the transference of consciousness, but I believe that the most important practice at the time of death is the awakening mind. That is what is most powerful. Although in my own daily practice I meditate on the process of death in association with various tantric practices seven or eight times a day, I still am convinced that I will find it easiest to remember the awakening mind when I die. That is the mind I really feel close to. Of course, by meditating on death, we also prepare ourselves for it, so we no longer need to worry about it. Although I am still not ready to face my actual death, I sometimes wonder how I will cope when actually faced with it. I am determined that if I live longer I will be able to accomplish much more. My will to live is equal to my excitement about facing death.

Remembering death is part of Buddhist practice. There are different aspects to this. One is to meditate constantly about death as a means for enhancing detachment from this life and its attractions. Another aspect is to rehearse the process of death, to familiarize yourself with the different levels of mind that are experienced as you die. When coarser levels of mind cease, the subtler mind comes to the fore. Meditating on the process of death is important in order to gain deeper experience of the subtle mind.

Death means that this body has certain limits. When the body can no longer be sustained, we die and take on a new body. The basic being or self that is designated onto the combination of body and mind persists after death, although the particular body is no more. The subtle body remains. From that point of view, the being has no beginning or no end; it will remain until Buddhahood.

Nevertheless, people are afraid of death. Unless you can guarantee your future due to your positive actions during this lifetime, there is every danger of being reborn in an unfavorable state of existence. In this lifetime, even if you lose your own country and become a refugee, you are still living in the human world. You can seek help and support. But after death you encounter entirely new circumstances. The ordinary experience we gain in this life is generally of no help after death. If you have not made proper preparations, things could be unfortunate. The way to prepare is by training the mind. On one level it means cultivating a sincere, compassionate motivation and performing positive actions, serving other sentient beings. At another level it means controlling your mind, which is a more profound way of preparing for the future. Eventually you can become master of your mind, which is the main purpose of meditation.

People who do not have any belief in anything after death would do better to think of death as just a part of life. Sooner or later we all have to face it. At least that will help us to think of death as something normal. Even if we deliberately avoid thinking about death, we cannot escape it. Faced with such a problem, you have two alternatives. One is simply not to think about it, to put it out of your mind. At least your mind will remain calm. But this is not a reliable option because the problem remains. Sooner or later you will have to face it. The other alternative is to face the problem, to think about it penetratingly. I know soldiers who say that their fear is greater before they fight than when they actually go into battle. If you think about death, your mind will become familiar with the idea. When it actually takes place it will be less of a shock and you will be less upset. Therefore, I think it is useful to think and talk about death.

We need to make our lives meaningful. In the scriptures, the realms of existence are described as impermanent, like a cloud in the autumn sky. The birth and death of human beings can be understood by watching the comings and goings of participants in a drama. You see the actors first in one costume and then in another. Within a short period of time, they undergo many changes. Our existence is also like that. The ebbing away of the human life is compared to lightning in the sky and the fall of a boulder down a steep incline. Water always runs downhill. It is impossible that it will ever run uphill. Almost without our noticing it, our lives run out. Those of us who accept the value of spiritual practice may think about our future lives, but in our hearts we focus principally on the purposes of this life alone. This is how we become confused and entrapped in the cycle of existence. We waste our lives. Right from the time of our birth we are approaching death. Yet we spend our lives mainly amassing food, clothing, and friends. At the time of death we have to leave them all behind. We have to travel to the next world alone, unaccompanied. The only thing that will benefit us is if we have undertaken some spiritual practice and have left some positive imprints within our minds. If we are to stop wasting our lives and provoke ourselves to do spiritual practice, we have to meditate on impermanence and our own mortality, the fact that from the moment of our birth our bodies are naturally impermanent and subject to disintegration.

Engaging in spiritual practices is not meant just to benefit this life, but to bring peace and happiness in the lives after death. One thing that hampers our practice is our tendency to think that we will live for a long time. We are like someone who has decided to settle down in a certain place. Such a person naturally becomes involved in the affairs of the world, amassing wealth, constructing buildings, planting crops, and so forth. On the other hand, the person who is more concerned about his or her lives after death is like a person who wants to travel. A traveler makes preparations to meet every eventuality and successfully reach his or her destination. As a result of death meditation, a practitioner becomes less obsessed with the affairs of this life: name and fame, possessions, social status. While working to meet the needs of this life, someone who meditates on death finds the time to generate the energy that can bring about peace and joy in future lives.

It is helpful to learn about the advantages of doing death meditation and the disadvantages of ignoring it. First, it is meditation on impermanence and death that inspires you to engage in spiritual practices. It is an eye-opener. When you become aware that sooner or later you have to leave this world, you are bound to be concerned about the affairs of the next life. This awareness automatically helps you to turn to spiritual pursuits. Second, death meditation is a powerful technique that helps you to prolong and continue your spiritual practice. In any endeavor of substance, be it spiritual or temporal, difficulties and problems are bound to occur. The power of death meditation helps you to face whatever hardships may come your way. Finally, this meditation acts as a stimulus, helping you to successfully complete your practice. Therefore, awareness of death is essential at every stage of your spiritual life. As a practitioner, you will be more concerned about the affairs of the life after death. And by eliminating deluded thoughts and actions, you will be able to make this life meaningful.

There are many disadvantages in not remembering death. When you forget death, there is very little chance of your being inclined toward practice. Without awareness of death, your practice will become slack and ineffective. You will be predominantly occupied with the affairs of this life. There are people who receive vows and recite their prayers daily. But because their awareness of death is weak, they behave like ordinary people in times of crisis, becoming excessively angry, attached, or jealous. There is a saying in Tibetan: "When you are well fed and enjoying the sunshine, you look like a practitioner. But when faced with a crisis you reveal your true nature." Everyday experience tells us that most of us are like this.

Without awareness of death, you have the affairs of this life at the centre of your heart. And because you are obsessed with wealth, status, and fame, you barely flinch when committing negative actions. A person who is not concerned about death naturally has no interest in the lives beyond it. Such an individual has no great regard for spiritual values and readily cultivates deluded thoughts and actions. Consequently, such a person is a source of harm to himself and others.

If you forget that you will die, you will think mainly about how to lead a prosperous life. Your most important concern will be to get a good place to stay, good clothes to wear, and good food to eat. You will not hesitate to deceive and threaten others if you get the chance. What is more, you might judge such negative activities as the marks of an efficient and capable person. This is a clear indication that you are not farsighted enough to think about the long future ahead. We all have many lives to come, which are completely dark to us and about which we have no idea. When you forget these circumstances, you will be inclined to pursue destructive activities.

Think of Hitler and Mao Tse-tung on the one hand and our spiritual forefathers, Milarepa and Tsong-kha-pa, on the other. They were all the same in that they were human beings, with human life and intelligence. But now, people like Mao and Hitler are regarded with deep disdain. People are shocked at the extent of their negative activities. On the other hand, when people think about the great Tibetan yogis, Milarepa and Tsong-kha-pa, they look to them for inspiration, they pray to them with faith and devotion. Although they had the same human potential, we think of them differently because of their activities. In the case of Hitler and Mao, human intelligence was used for destructive purposes. In the case of Milarepa and Tsong-kha-pa, it was used constructively.

If we let our minds be controlled by disturbing emotions, they will bring destruction for many lives to come. Consequently, we will die full of regret. While we are alive we may seem to be good practitioners, but actually our lives are empty of real practice. A story is told of someone who was supposed to be a spiritual practitioner. He used to boast that when he died, he would definitely take birth in a pure realm. Then he fell fatally ill. It was certain he was going to die, but his close friends said: "It is no problem for you. You are going to take birth in a pure realm. But what about us? We have neither support nor friends." Then the apparent practitioner said, "It would be better if we didn't have to die at all." So on his deathbed, instead of thinking about the pure realm, he was lamenting his impending death.

Awareness of death can be developed through both formal and analytical meditation. You must first understand the certainty of death intellectually. It is not some obscure theoretical issue, but an obvious and observable fact. Our world is believed to be some 5 billion years old, and the human race has been in existence for the last one hundred thousand years. Over such a long period of time, is there even one human being who did not have to face death? Death is absolutely inevitable regardless of where you live, whether you hide deep in the ocean or fly up into the open sky.

It makes no difference who you are, you have to die. Stalin and Mao were two of the most powerful men of our own century. Nevertheless, they too had to die, and it appears that they faced death with fear and unhappiness. When they were alive they ruled as dictators. They were surrounded by attendants and lackeys ready to do their bidding. They ruled ruthlessly, ready to destroy anything that challenged their authority. But when they were faced with death, everyone that they had trusted up to that point, everything they had relied on, their power, their weapons, their military force, were no longer of any use. Under such circumstances anyone would feel afraid. The advantage of developing awareness of death is that it will help you make your life meaningful. You will regard the enduring peace and happiness as more important than short-term pleasure. Recollecting death is like using a hammer to destroy all negative tendencies and disturbing emotions.

When we recall the names and wonderful deeds of all the teachers from the compassionate Buddha Shakyamuni right up to the contemporary lamas who have passed away, we might feel that they are still with us. But when we investigate, all of them have entered into nirvana. If we go to look for them now, all we will find are some relics, a few handfuls of ashes or bones. With regard even to the Buddha himself, all we can find are bones and relics in certain pilgrimage places. And when you see them you feel like crying.

None of the saintly scholars of ancient India is alive today. We can only read about their lives in the pages of history books. They are now no more than a record, a fragment of memory. The great kings and emperors of the ancient world, who enjoyed unprecedented power over their citizens, were all powerless when faced with death. Every one of them succumbed to their final fate. Reflecting on history brings home the fact that death is imminent and universal. Impermanence is real. Recognizing that will motivate us to become better practitioners. All of the world's great leaders, those who were loved and respected by their citizens and the notoriously powerful who were feared and hated, had to die. None of them could cheat death. Compare this to your own situation. You have friends, relatives, and family. Some had already died and you had to cope with that sadness. Sooner or later others too will face the same fate.

One hundred years from now, people may say that the Dalai Lama gave teachings in this place. But none of us here will still exist, whether the buildings have fallen into ruin or remain standing. Death has no respect for seniority or age. It is more like a random lottery. Generally, we expect the old to go first and the younger to follow. But there are so many cases of children and grandchildren who die, leaving their parents to do the last rites. If we had the power, we should pass a law banning the lord of death from taking the lives of the young. They have not had enough time to enjoy the world. But it is a law of nature that there is nothing definite about who will go first and who will stay behind. If we could take the lord of death to court, we would surely do so. Yet, no military power can capture death. The richest person cannot buy death off, and the most cunning person cannot deceive death by trickery.

There is not one of us who does not cherish himself or herself. We do everything we can to take care of ourselves. In order to enjoy good health and lead a long life, we take regular meals and exercise. Even when we fall slightly ill, we visit a doctor and take his medicine. We also perform religious rituals to ward off interferences and difficulties. Despite all this, death will come for us all one day. When death strikes, no one else can help. You may have your head in the Buddha's lap and the Medicine Buddha may be here to treat you, but when death strikes even they are helpless. When your life-span is exhausted, you have to go. It is not hard to understand the certainty of death. Our life-spans are ticking away no matter where or who we are. With every twenty-four hours another day is gone. With every thirty days a month is gone, and with twelve months a year is complete. This is how our lives will come to an end.

Unless you make a special effort yourself to do spiritual practice and lead a life in accordance with the Dharma, merely being alive is not a guarantee of practice. For the first twenty years of our lives we say we are young and do not engage in practice. Then we pass another twenty years saying, "I will practice, I will practice," but we do not do so. Then we pass another twenty years saying, "I couldn't do it, I couldn't do it," lamenting that we cannot study because we are too old, our sight is not good, and we can't hear properly. This is how we waste our lives. The strange thing is that although our physical bodies soon get sick, old, and worn out, the disturbing emotions within us remain fresh. They never age. Sexual desire may diminish as we grow old, but the rest of the disturbing emotions remain strong.

As children and in our youth we pass our time playing. As a child I too had many playmates, particularly among the sweepers working in my residence. At that time another friend tried to quiz me about the different colors, topics dealt with in the preliminary studies of logic. I did not know the answers then, because I was quite young. I became annoyed and determined to study hard. When I was fifteen or sixteen years old, I started thinking about the *Stages of the Path to Enlightenment*, but the invasion of the Chinese interrupted my studies. Until I was twenty-four or twenty-five I tried to do some spiritual practice, but at the same time I was always trying to negotiate with the Chinese. I was twenty-five when I became a refugee and came into exile. I studied quite hard in my late twenties and early thirties. Thirty-five years have passed since I came into exile, and I am now in my sixties.

I had a great intention to do practice, but this is how my life has turned out. My only consolation is that the omniscient Gendun Gyatso, the second Dalai Lama, also saw his good intentions disrupted. He oversaw the construction of the main temple at Tashilhunpo and taught his students at the same time. In his biography you can read how busy he was. One of his students once told him, "I would like to retire to the mountains and do some serious practice." He replied, sadly, "When I was staying in the Kangchen hermitage I had fewer demands on my time. I feel that if I had stayed in retreat there, by now I might have achieved great realization. But I turned down the opportunity out of a wish to benefit as many people as possible. This was my motivation for establishing Tashilhunpo Monastery." This is some consolation to me, for although I am unable to do a thorough practice of recitation, prayer, and retreat, I try to benefit others as much as possible. Of course I am doing some practice, but I am unable to put all my energy into it because of other preoccupations. What I can tell you is that if you think of practice in a relaxed way, continuing to enjoy everything else, it is really difficult to achieve anything.

Gampopa stayed a long time with Milarepa receiving all his instructions and meditating on them. When the time came for him to depart, Milarepa said, "I have still one instruction to give to you, but it may not be proper to give it to you now." Gampopa replied, "Please give me that instruction. Whatever instruction you have, please give it to me." But Milarepa declined and Gampopa set out on his own way. Then Milarepa called out, "Just wait, since you are like my only son, I will give you the last instruction." So saying, he lifted his robe and showed Gampopa his calloused backside, a sign of his having undergone intense practice seated in meditation. He added, "If you really persist, you too should achieve Buddhahood. We always boast about the potential of the Dharma and that we can achieve Buddhahood in one lifetime, but whether it is possible or not depends upon how hard you work."

In developing awareness of death, you need next to think about how unpredictable it is. This is expressed by a popular saying: "Tomorrow or the next life, you never know which will come first." We all know death will come one day. The problem is that we always think it will be some time in the future. We are always busy with our worldly affairs. Therefore, it is essential to meditate on death's unpredictability. Traditional texts explain that the life-span of the people of this world is uncertain, particularly in this degenerate age. Death does not follow any rule or order. Anyone can die any time, whether they are old or young, rich or poor, sickly or well. Nothing can be taken for granted in relation to death. Strong, healthy people die suddenly due to unforeseen circumstances, while weak, bedridden patients hang on for a long time.

Comparing the causes that can lead to death with the limited factors that help sustain life, we can see why death is unpredictable. We hold this human body dear, believing that it is strong and will last a long time. But reality defies our hopes. Compared with rock and steel, our bodies are feeble and delicate. We eat to maintain our health and sustain our lives, but there are occasions when even food makes us sick and leads to our death. Nothing can guarantee that we will live forever.

The achievements of modern science and technology are clear expressions of our human desire for a better and fuller life. But we cling to new gadgets as if they were life-sustaining tools. Cars, trains, ships, and aircraft are meant to improve our lives and provide comfort and convenience. Yet, so often these things bring us physical and mental trouble. The death toll due to road accidents is high everywhere. What does this imply about our desire to travel safely and fast? People die instantly and without any warning. Despite our efforts to create safety and security, our life is fraught with peril. We never know when death will strike.

Death is dreaded as the end of life. To make matters worse, nothing that we work for in this life—wealth, power, fame, friends, or family—can help at that time. You may be a powerful person backed by a huge military force, but when death strikes it cannot defend you. You may be wealthy and able to buy the best care when you are sick, but when death finally prevails, there is not expert you can hire who can forestall death. When you have to leave the world, your wealth stays behind. You cannot take a single penny with you. Your dearest friend cannot accompany you. You have to face the next world alone. Only your experience of spiritual practice can help you.

Stalin and Mao were very powerful leaders. Security around them was tight, so ordinary people did not have easy access to them. I vividly remember meeting Mao in the same hall every time during my stay in Beijing. Security guards stood at the doors and watched us constantly. But when death strikes, such security is worthless. Similarly, I believe there are people prepared to sacrifice their lives for the security of the Dalai Lama. But when death finally catches up with me, I will be on my own. Being the Dalai Lama will not help. If I protest that I am a monk with disciples and followers, that too will not help.

Now think about the millionaire. At the point of death, his wealth only adds to his pain and misery. During those last moments, the wealthy person worries intensely. Things are slipping out of his control. On top of the physical discomfort, the mind is more confused than ever. Thinking about how to distribute his wealth and whom to give it to only increases the anguish. This is not some obscure philosophical speculation, but a daily occurrence. It is essential to meditate on these matters in order to realize that at the time of death and after death, wealth in any form proves utterly worthless.

While you are alive, friends and relatives play a great role in shaping your destiny. Accordingly, you treat them as important and generate warm feelings toward them. Some are so dear to your heart that you feel you could not survive without them. But when you are about to die, they too are helpless. Some of them may be ready to do anything for you. But on this occasion, they are literally powerless. All they can do is pray for your future lives. Indeed, instead of being of any help, friends and relatives can cause great pain and distress to a dying person. Even when you are lying exhausted on your deathbed, anxiety about the future of your family can cause you intense pain. You worry about what will happen to them after your death.

Your own body is very precious to you. It has been your most reliable, firmest companion since your very conception. You have done all you can to give it the best care. You have fed it so that it will not be hungry. You have given it drink when it was thirsty. You have rested when it was tired. You have been prepared to do anything and everything for the care, comfort, and protection of your body. In fairness, your body has also served you. It has always been ready to fulfill your needs. Just the function of the heart is a source of amazement. It is constantly at work. It literally never stops, whatever you do, whether you are asleep or awake. But when death strikes, your body gives up. Your consciousness and your body separate, and your precious body becomes simply a dreadful corpse. Thus, in the face of death, your wealth and possessions, friends and relatives, and even your own body can do you no good. The only thing that can help you face the unknown is the virtue you have planted on the stream of your consciousness. This is why spiritual practice can help you make your life meaningful.

By and large, people are not very interested in discussing death. But it does not go away simply because we close our eyes and turn our minds away from it. Regardless of our circumstances, we all have to face it one day. So in order to prepare ourselves in advance, it is useful to meditate on the process of dying. This means imagining what it is like to die. We can make this crucial situation fresh and personal by means of meditation. If it is to have full impact, you should meditate on the process of dying following your meditation on the certainty of death. This will lend force to your meditation on the unpredictability of death.

As we have already discussed, death can occur at any time. There is no particular juncture at which someone has to undergo the process of dying. Death occurs when a person's life-span or the force of his or her virtue is exhausted. Or it can take place as a sudden accident. You might initially fall ill. You naturally consult a doctor, who prescribes certain treatment. But this time things turn out differently; the treatment proves ineffective. Then you might perform rituals and prayers. This too may make some difference, but with time you become more ill. To make matters worse, your doctor cannot come to a clear diagnosis because your sickness keeps making twists and turns. This naturally prolongs your problem. After you have to be in bed a long time, sick and exhausted, your chances of recovery become ever more bleak. Even the soft bed gives you discomfort. After so much suffering, parts of your body become numb like a corpse.

What goes on in the mind of the dying? After you have been sick and bedridden for a long time, the power of your mind becomes slack. You may have been an active and sharp-witted person, but now your brain has become dull and you suffer lapses of memory. There are times when you cannot remember even the names of the people around you. At times the pain is so excruciating you are not able to say even a little prayer. Under such depression you begin to lose hope, which directly affects your will and determination to live. Then you also begin to wonder if there is no cure and why you should suffer such pain and misery. You decide you have no other option but to die. Your family and friends lament that you are neither dying nor getting better. It becomes increasingly difficult to attract anyone's attention.

Gradually your body loses its heat and becomes as stiff as a log. As great teachers of the past have said, your last meal is some blessed pills or medicines you can hardly swallow. The last words you hear may be the chanting of scriptures or cries of lamentation. There are no good words to say. If you have been wealthy, you might still be worrying about your estate; your mind might be filled with worries about the money people owe you or the ways of dividing your wealth among your relatives and friends. You are filled with inexpressible anxiety and pain. You try to utter a few last words, which are barely audible. By the time your power of speech has failed, only your lips can be seen to twitch. The very sight is sad and pitiable.

Under these deplorable circumstances, the elements of your body gradually start to fail. You are haunted by various hallucinations. You may feel as if you were being submerged under the earth or falling from a height, or you may have sensations of burning. As the liquid element fails, your eyes and nose become depressed and pinched. Your tongue becomes dry. As the solid element fails, your body becomes thin. As the heat element fails, your body becomes cold. As your energy fails, you lose the ability to move and you find it hard to breathe. You begin to pant short and fast, until with a long exhalation you release your last breath like a violin string breaking. The heart stops, and within a matter of minutes, the brain too ceases to function. You are now considered clinically dead.

According to modern science, after breathing ceases and the heart stops beating, the function of the brain stops within minutes. However, according to the Buddhist explanation there are still another four stages to go. There are no more external indications, only internal signs or feelings. At each stage you see different colored lights. First whitish, then reddish, then darkness, and finally, there is a feeling of infinite space, which is known as the "clear light." Although the grosser levels of consciousness have ceased to exist, the subtle consciousness has not departed from the body. The ability to stay with the clear light normally belongs only to highly evolved meditators, but occasionally people become absorbed in it accidentally. One of the best examples of a highly realized meditator who remained absorbed in the clear light was my own senior tutor, Ling Rinpoche. For thirteen days he remained in that state, during which time the luster and freshness of his body remained.

In life you face hardship to amass food and wealth, but at death you have to leave it. Who knows how your wealth will be used by those who inherit it? For a few days they may grieve for you, but soon they will be squabbling over their share. This is how your life is spent. If you visit a cemetery or crematorium, look at how bodies are disposed of and reflect that they are no different from you. That too is a way to meditate on impermanence. However, just because you have died, you do not disappear like a burning heap of dry grass; your continuity goes on. Whether your next rebirth is in a favorable or unfavorable state of existence depends on the kind of virtuous practices you have done. Can you be confident of taking birth in a favorable state of existence?

If we do not reflect about the imminence of death, we will not recall our spiritual practice. The path is our guide for traveling to an unknown place. In ordinary life too, if we want to go somewhere we have not been before, we are careful to seek the guidance of someone who has been there. We take a map with us. We plan where to stop, where to stay, and what to take for the journey. But when it comes to going to the unknown place called the next life, the ordinary experiences we have gathered in this life are of little use. Our only guide is our practice. That does not mean that we carry a lot of scriptures along with us, but that our minds should be thoroughly prepared and transformed.

What kind of practice will help us when we travel to that unknown place? Positive deeds are something we can trust forever. The useful method here is to observe the ten virtuous qualities and refrain from the ten unwholesome deeds. If we are able to leave positive imprints on our minds, and if we are able in particular to generate a very positive state of mind at the time of death, then we can be confident of taking a favorable rebirth. The kind of rebirth we take depends upon the kind of actions we have done. And whichever action we latch onto at the time of death will project its effect first.

Remembering the awakening mind automatically brings calmness and peace of mind at the time of death. Cultivating a virtuous state of mind as you die can cause virtuous action to ripen and ensure a good rebirth. Therefore, from the point of view of a Buddhist practitioner, living a meaningful daily life means making yourself familiar with virtuous states of mind, which will eventually help you face death. Whether your experience at the time of death is positive or negative is very much dependent on how you have practiced during your life. The important thing is that our day-to-day life should be meaningful, that our attitude should be positive, happy, and warm.

CHAPTER 3

Living with Purpose

The great master Gungthang said that this precious life as a free and fortunate human being can be obtained just once. Even though we have had countless lives in the past, we have never yet been able to put such a precious human life to proper use. Today, we are fortunate to have found a life in which our mental and physical faculties are intact, and we have some interest in practicing the Dharma. Such a life is unique. Similarly, the Dharma we have access to is unique. It first derived from the Buddha in India, and it was passed down by subsequent great Indian masters. Gradually it came to flourish in Tibet, and that tradition of Buddhist practice is still very much alive. In Tibet, the Land of Snows, we have maintained the complete range of practice of the teachings of the Buddha. Therefore, at this time it is extremely important that we make a concerted effort to use it to fulfill the best purposes of ourselves and all other sentient beings.

Although we have all obtained a precious life as a human being, we enjoy it without recognizing its value. At the same time we do not recognize the limitations of other forms of life in which there is no opportunity to appreciate the teaching. The animals and birds who surround us have no capacity to understand such a precious teaching. Even as human beings, if we had been born as one of those people who have no interest in such teachings, we would ignore them as animals do. More sensitive people might think that there is some reason to listen to the teachings, but would not engage in study and contemplation beyond that. We are extremely fortunate. We have not been born in uncivilized lands where there is no practice of Buddhism. We are free from major hindrances. Having obtained such a very precious opportunity, we must recognize its value and potential.

Even people running small businesses know that there is a time and place for doing business. They know that if they try to sell their goods out of season they will fail. Likewise, a farmer is aware of trends in the weather and does not hesitate to cultivate his land when the time comes, even if he has to work day and night. Likewise, as free and fortunate human beings we have this rare opportunity and the time to make the utmost use of it.

Of course, when I talk about the importance of Dharma practice, I am not trying to force anyone to do it. Trying to force someone to do anything, even something worthwhile, is of no use. The most important Buddhist practice is mental transformation, and it is for the sake of mental transformation that we engage in contemplation and meditation. Meditation is a means of familiarizing ourselves with positive aspects of the mind. And in this way we try to tame our unruly, disobedient minds. The mind certainly can be trained. Take the example of training a horse. In the beginning, the horse may be wild and difficult to handle, but gradually we can tame it until it obeys our commands. Likewise in the initial stage, when we are not used to mental training, our minds are so addicted to negative habits that they are difficult to control and go their own way. If we meditate and familiarize ourselves with positive qualities, we can gradually train and transform the mind. Therefore, meditation is a means for changing our mental attitude and making the mind more positive.

When we think again and again about the value of human life and the rare opportunity it presents, we become convinced of the need to make use of it to transform our minds and eventually attain enlightenment. We have to meditate, which means that we make our minds totally familiar with the topic of meditation, such as compassion. In this way we can transform our minds so that, for example, as soon as we think about the sufferings of sentient beings, we will be moved to take responsibility for helping them. Through familiarity we become accustomed to positive activities. This kind of contemplation and reflection is called analytical meditation.

When we meet people for the first time, we do not recognize their different expressions, attitudes, or habits. But as we gradually get to know them, we become accustomed to our friends' ways. If we associate with good friends, we will gradually pick up their good qualities. Under the influence of good friends we can also reduce our negative behavior, because we will be careful not to do anything which will displease them. Within our consciousness, there are countless varieties of mind. These countless aspects of the mind belong to three major categories: those that are neutral, those that are beneficial and positive, and those that are negative and harmful. We need to grow accustomed to positive states of mind and be influenced by them, just as we get to know good friends. We have to cultivate the positive aspects of the mind, those which are beneficial to us. This is like gardening or farming. We cultivate those flowers and plants that are useful, but we discard weeds.

When we talk about creating something of spiritual value in our minds, we have to make effort personally by using the mind itself. Our mental defects must be reduced and weakened, and the positive qualities of the mind must be developed and cultivated. First we must establish which aspects of the mind are positive and which are destructive or negative. We can appreciate and cultivate the positive aspects. With negative states of the mind like anger, jealousy, competitiveness, and attachment, we need to understand why they are negative, how they arise in us, and how they leave us disturbed and unhappy. Understanding their drawbacks will help us reduce them. It is not enough simply to say that these negative states of the mind are negative because the scriptures say so. We must examine our own experience to find out how destructive and negative these states of mind are.

For example, when we get angry and express our anger violently and harshly, we are likely to say something nasty to others. At that time we are actually mad, we lose our sense of discrimination. The expression on our faces is horrible and ugly. Clearly, such behavior is disturbing. Are families who continually quarrel happier? Are those places where there is constant conflict and fighting happier? Obviously not. If we are unexpectedly visited by a hot-tempered person, we may not feel like making him or her welcome, but if we are visited by a jolly, compassionate person, we immediately ask them to sit down and offer them tea. We can easily identify the negativity of anger, jealousy, and competitiveness in others.

Of all the negative aspects of the mind, it is basically anger, attachment, and competitiveness that are responsible for other negative states of the mind. Once we can recognize the negativity of these mental states, we will be able to recognize their warning signs when they occur. Such analytical processes can help us guide our minds in a positive direction. This kind of practice is very effective and useful. When we talk about meditation, we tend to think of meditators sitting high up in the mountains. Dharma practice is about transforming the mind, and it is only through repeated meditation and familiarization that you can transform your mind. It is something we can all do, wherever we are.

When we come to a conclusion through analytical meditation and start to gain insight into the object of our meditation, we should try to let our minds remain there single-pointedly for a while. Through this combination of analytical meditation and single-pointed concentration, we can gradually transform our minds. This is much more effective than reciting hundreds of prayers. In this way we will be able to make our precious human life meaningful. If instead you simply procrastinate, thinking that you will start tomorrow, next month, or next year, time will run out. If you think that you will be able to practice only after you have completed a particular project or you have gotten everything else out of the way, the time will never come. It is said that the more worldly activities you start, the more there are, like unceasing waves on the sea. Would it not be better just to stop and begin to practice the Dharma?

When I was young I only had to do some memorization and some recitation. I had a lot of time but little interest. When I was in my twenties I made some effort and was able to gain some understanding of the reality of nirvana. I expected to do a major retreat, a three-year-three-month retreat, but I became more and more busy and could not find the time. Nowadays, even though I am busy, I make myself create the opportunity and do whatever practice I can.

Even ordained monks and nuns in their simple rooms always have something else to do. A time will never come when you are free of all activities, so every day you have to find the opportunity. You have to get up slightly earlier and try to find one or two hours in the morning for your meditation practice. If you say you will do your practice when you have completed all your work, it is a sign that you are not really willing to do any Dharma practice. Therefore, the great Gungthang said that if you want to practice the Dharma, never say that you will do it tomorrow or the day after tomorrow. Start doing it today. If you say that you will practice the Dharma tomorrow, there is every likelihood that before that tomorrow comes you will die. Death is definite but the time of death is indefinite—it can strike us at any time, therefore do not procrastinate.

Traditionally we are advised outwardly to observe monastic discipline, inwardly to meditate on the awakening mind, and secretly to practice the two stages of the path of tantra. It is extremely important to practice the Dharma when we are young, when both body and mind are fresh and energetic. It is particularly important to do tantric practice when we are young, when the psychic channels and energies within them are fresh. Generally, when people become old they suffer the sickness of old age, and their memories become weak. But it is noticeable that people who studied and meditated in their youth have fresh, agile, and active minds in their old age. If, when we are young, we do certain deity yoga practices and practices like transference of consciousness, because of the power of habituation we will be able to recall these practices at the time of death. At that time, we will be able to focus our minds on these practices. Therefore, from the point of view of doing meditation on the complete path, it is important to start when you are young. As a great practitioner you will welcome death, as a moderate practitioner you will not fear death, and even as an inferior practitioner, you will have nothing to regret at the time of death.

To begin with, we purify our unwholesome deeds by admitting them openly. Appealing to the Buddhas and bodhisattvas abiding in the ten directions, we admit that from beginningless time, revolving in the cycle of existence in this and other lives, we have done negative deeds and instigated others to do so because of our ignorance. Seeing them as mistakes, we confess and regret them.

Why do we confess our unwholesome deeds? Because otherwise there is every likelihood of death overtaking us before we have the chance to do so. Therefore, we ask the objects of refuge to give us protection and help us to liberate ourselves from the consequences of our unwholesome deeds. We must confess them quickly and purify them quickly, because death is unpredictable. Death does not wait to see whether we have completed what we planned to do. Death never holds back and allows someone to live longer because he or she has not accumulated enough virtuous deeds. It makes no difference whether we are sick or healthy; death never waits. Death may snatch away our lives while we are unprepared.

Life is fleeting and unreliable. We have to leave behind our relatives and our possessions. Unaware of this, we have accumulated negative deeds, physically, verbally, and mentally, in relation to those who are close to us and those who are not so close. Whether they are friendly or unfriendly, they too will soon disappear. Our so-called enemy will also die. Our so-called friends will also die. This is certain. Not only that: we, who have accumulated an abundance of positive and negative deeds in relation to such friends and enemies, will also disappear. Our friends and relatives, our enemies and wealth—everything is transient, impermanent, and will all finally disappear. A time will come when we will be unable to see them or hear them. When we think about them they will be just something we remember. We will feel as if all these things happened in a dream. All conditioned phenomena, the whole environment, and whatever you have enjoyed, all will be just something vaguely remembered.

However, the unwholesome deeds we have accumulated will remain behind. Even though many of our friends and enemies have died, the negative deeds we accumulated in relation to them will always abide in our minds as long as we do not adopt antidotes to purify and remove them. The disturbing emotions and the negative deeds they gave rise to will remain fresh in our minds until we purify them.

Because we have never understood our fleeting nature, we have never understood that we are only going to live for a short time. Because of this lack of realization, out of ignorance, attachment, and hatred, we have engaged in various kinds of unwholesome deeds. We have displayed indifference toward neutral sentient beings, attachment toward friends, and anger, jealousy, and hatred toward our enemies. We have accumulated negative deeds like these for a long time. At the same time, our lives have been ebbing away and coming to an end. The day will not wait, the night will not wait. Minute by minute, second by second, time is being consumed and our lives are ebbing away. Our lives are constantly approaching their ends.

At the end the only source of refuge is whatever merit you have accumulated. If you have observed morality, have practiced the ten virtuous qualities, and have cultivated some genuine compassion, you may have some powerful virtuous quality within your mind. It is only that virtuous quality that will help you. No one else can help you, and there will be no one to whom you can turn for help. But since your own mind is not hidden from you, you may find that you have not collected any of these virtuous qualities. You will lament, "Unconscientiously, carelessly, unaware of such a frightening state as this, being attracted and deceived by fleeting pleasures, I have done countless negative deeds for the sake of this fleeting impermanent life. I have wasted my life in meaningless activity."

The actual refuge is the Dharma. We take refuge in the Buddhas and bodhisattvas, but, as it is said in the scriptures, the Buddhas do not wash away the negative deeds of sentient beings. The Buddhas cannot remove the sufferings of sentient beings with their hands; they cannot transfer their realizations into the minds of other sentient beings. It is only by being shown the truth of reality that sentient beings are liberated. Therefore, we take refuge in the actual protector, which is the Dharma. We say, "In the past I have transgressed your instructions. Now that I have seen what there is to fear, I take refuge in you. Please calm my fears quickly."

Therefore, we need to rely on the practice of the Dharma. Even when we are afflicted by an ordinary sickness, we have to pay heed to the doctor's instructions. So, afflicted as we are by hundreds of disturbing emotions like attachment, what need is there to talk about taking refuge in the Dharma, the instructions of the physicianlike Buddha? There is no medicine to cure the disturbing emotions; the only remedy is the instruction and teaching of the Buddha. Nothing else can remove the disturbing emotions from the root.

In this century, during World War I and World War II, many people were killed. There was the mass execution of Jews by the Nazis, the extermination of millions under Stalin. Similarly, millions died under Mao's regime. All these deaths were due to the disturbing emotions within the mind of the person who ordered them. When we do not know how to check our disturbing emotions by applying antidotes, the disturbing emotions take their own course. The result can be incredible destruction. Therefore, it is absolutely true to say that even one kind of disturbing emotion can destroy all the human beings in the world. All the troubles, suffering, and uneasiness that we experience in this world are due to disturbing emotions.

All excellent qualities, all happiness, result from this mind wishing to benefit other people. Whether it is a positive worldly achievement or a spiritual achievement, all good qualities come through having a mind wishing to benefit other sentient beings. Whether we accept a particular religious practice or not, all of us need to make an effort to be warm-hearted. If we can manage that, we will all experience peace and happiness. Don't we feel better if someone greets us with a smile? And don't we feel badly when someone growls and frowns at us? We are social animals; we live in a society in which the very basis of our existence is cooperation and mutual dependence. Cooperation is founded on an attitude of loving-kindness toward each other. If we have that, there will be peace and happiness within our families, within our neighborhoods, and within society at large. On the other hand, if we are always plotting against each other, harboring resentment toward each other, we may have an abundance of material facilities at our disposal, but we will have no happiness.

Under totalitarian systems, there are spies to pry into every activity within the community, even within the family. As a result, people lose trust in each other and constantly remain suspicious and full of doubt. Once we have lost a basic sense of trust and sincere appreciation for each other, how can we expect to find happiness? Instead we will live in a society racked by fear and suspicion, like a crow who is afraid even of his own shadow.

Therefore, a mind wishing to benefit other people and other sentient beings is the very basis of peace and happiness. Today, in many developed countries there is a degree of material and technological progress. But due to a lack of inner peace, inner compassion, those countries continue to face a host of problems. It is a great mistake to think that only money can bring satisfaction and contentment. Altruism or a mind wishing to benefit other sentient beings definitely plays a part.

Due to technological developments, the destructive potential of modern warfare is beyond our imagination. Of course, we say that we have to wage war to bring about peace. But how can we establish lasting peace and happiness on the basis of war, anger, and bullying others? Real cooperation, real lasting peace and happiness can be brought about only on the basis of compassion and loving-kindness. Whenever I travel abroad and talk to different people, I always stress the importance of a good mind, and mind wishing to benefit others. In the Buddhist scriptures, the main emphasis is on the cultivation of altruism. It is a unique kind of altruism, because the focus is on how to cultivate the mind wishing to attain Buddhahood for the sake of all suffering sentient beings.

In order to cultivate altruism and the awakening mind, meditation is essential. In order for meditation to be successful, it is important to know how to prepare to meditate. We first prepare a comfortable seat and arrange an altar. Then we sit, observing the proper posture, and reflect on the four immeasurable wishes: love, wishing that sentient beings have happiness; compassion, wishing that they be free from suffering; joy in their abiding forever in bliss; and the equanimity free of attachment and aversion. We visualize the merit field and offer a mandala representing the entire universe. Then we make supplications and receive blessings.

These kinds of preparatory practices must be done as an important part of whatever meditation we do. First we have to make the place where we are going to practice clean and comfortable. At the same time we need to be cautious that we do not give rise to the eight worldly concerns: gain and loss, pleasure and pain, praise and blame, fame and disrepute. When we arrange the altar and set up images, we should pay equal respect to the images of Buddhas and bodhisattvas, regardless of their aesthetic quality or the material from which they are made.

The Buddha has no weapons in his hands; he is just a compassionate monk. One of the scriptures on logic illustrates the Buddha's all-embracing compassion. It describes two people sitting on either side of him, one paying him respect and anointing him with sandalwood oil, the other cutting away his flesh with a sharp knife. Yet the Buddha does not differentiate between the two. He has no special friends to care for and no special enemies to be eliminated. The Buddha tamed the host of negative forces just prior to his enlightenment without using sharp weapons or missiles; his only implements were compassion and love. Thinking of this, I cannot help praising the amazing qualities of the Buddha.

When we arrange the altar we should arrange the images properly in their respective order and place whatever articles of offering we have before them. The offerings should be pure and should have been obtained by honest means. We should not think of any of these things just as material goods, as items for commerce. For example, it is reprehensible to sell scriptures, statues, or stupas simply for the sake of filling your stomach. On the other hand, to distribute certain rare scriptures and use any proceeds for further publication is acceptable. Nowadays I hear that in Tibet there is some kind of trade in images and other things involving smuggling, and I feel very sad about this.

To help us cultivate the jewel-like awakening mind we make offerings to the Buddhas, the Dharma, and the community of bodhisattvas, who possess infinite oceanlike qualities. We make offerings to them physically, verbally, and mentally. Because our own possessions are limited in extent and quality, we can mentally visualize making extensive offerings of flowers, fruit, medicinal substances, and precious jewels. We can imagine all those things in the world that have no owner: pure, clean water, mountains, forests, peaceful isolated places, clouds of incense, plants covered with beautiful flowers, trees laden with fruit, uncultivated crops, oceans, pools covered with lotus flowers, sweetly singing birds. We request the Buddhas, Dharma, and Spiritual Community to accept what we offer and to take care of us out of their compassion. We pay homage to places associated with the awakening mind, reliquaries housing scriptures, and so forth. We pay homage with speech by reciting prayers and praises, not out of fear or flattery but inspired by the mental homage of faith and admiration.

Physical admiration means that we bow down to the objects of refuge. We touch the five limbs of our body to the ground: both knees, the palms of both hands, and our forehead. Our outstretched palms must touch the ground, not simply our fists. Likewise, the forehead should touch the ground. This is how we make a half prostration. To make a full prostration we let our entire body down onto the ground like a felled tree. We should stretch out our arms and let both our hands entirely touch the ground. Our arms should not be splayed out like the limbs of a frog. Because it is said that the merit acquired by prostration depends on the amount of ground covered by the body, a famous lama from Chamdo, who was physically huge, would boast that his great body earned a huge stock of merit. Therefore, we should stretch ourselves out to fullest possible extent. Making full-length prostrations, lying down flat on the ground, is not an occasion to rest. We have to get up again quickly.

We fold our hands together, leaving a space between them as if we were holding a jewel. This empty space between our hands represents emptiness and the possibility of attaining the Buddha's Truth Body. Of course, emptiness does not mean total nothingness. It can also be explained as a state free from any kind of obstruction. So, the hollow between the hands and the shape formed by the hands symbolize the two bodies of the Buddha: the Truth Body and the Form Body, respectively.

With our hands folded in this way we touch the forehead, representing our physical actions, the throat, which is the site of our speech, and the heart. Consciousness may reside anywhere, but when we touch our hands at the heart, the center of the body, we are indicating the site of the indestructible energy, where the primordial mind resides. After having touched these three places of the body, we bow down and touch the ground.

When you next offer bowls of water to the Buddhas and bodhisattvas, you should not first set up a line of empty bowls. Pick them up in a stack and fill the bowl on top with water. Then, as you take the first one off the stack, pour the water into the next bowl, leaving a little water in it as you place it on the altar. Each bowl will then contain a little water when it is placed on the altar. When you then fill the bowls with water, pour it carefully with respect. Otherwise water will splash everywhere, which is not respectful. For example, when you offer your guests tea, you do not splash it all over the table. When we make these offerings, we are offering to higher, realized beings. The way we pour the water is described as being like the shape of a barley grain: thin and gentle at the beginning, thick and steady in the middle, and tapering off again at the end. We should also prepare a clean lamp. A kind old lama explained to me that when he prepared a very thick wick, the butter or oil in the lamp was soon finished and it produced a lot of smoke. When we burn a butter lamp it should look clean and tidy.

When we commit some unwholesome deed, we must repent. Milarepa said: "If you are wondering about the process for purifying unwholesome deeds, you must repent." We must cultivate a strong sense of restraint, which means making a determination to refrain from repeating our mistakes in the future. Reciting certain mantras, particularly the hundred-syllable mantra and confessional prayers, circumambulating the temple, and doing prostrations with this kind of motivation are powerful antidotes to purify negative deeds. Similarly, we can meditate on emptiness with a wish to purify negative deeds.

The next step is rejoicing. To rejoice means not to feel jealous or resentful of the virtuous deeds done by other Dharma practitioners. Instead, if we wholeheartedly admire other people's good practice, we will be able to accumulate great virtue. When we see someone accumulating the causes that lead to the attainment of a well-placed rebirth or we see someone who has attained such a status, it is a cause for rejoicing. Likewise, we should rejoice at the accumulation of merit that becomes a cause for attaining enlightenment. We should rejoice at the liberation of sentient beings from the sufferings of the cycle of existence through the practice of the three trainings. We should rejoice at the causes of the attainment of Buddhahood, the ten levels of the bodhisattvas, and the resulting state of Buddhahood itself. Likewise, the generation of the awakening mind, the mind wishing to benefit other sentient beings, the source of oceanic virtue that brings peace and happiness to all sentient beings, is a source of great joy.

The next step is making requests to the Buddhas to turn the wheel of the doctrine. With folded hands, which are a physical expression of supplication, we make requests to all the Buddhas of the ten directions. The minds of sentient beings are obscured by ignorance and suffering. In order to dispel this miserable darkness we request the Buddhas to light the lamp of Dharma. This is followed by requesting the Buddhas not to pass away into final nirvana. We request them not to forsake sentient beings, but to stay continuously in this world for countless eons to teach the Dharma to suffering sentient beings.

Finally, there is the dedication. Having performed all these virtuous activities in this way, we dedicate them, wishing that they all become a cause for dispelling the sufferings of countless sentient beings. We make elaborate wishes that until everyone who is sick is cured, we may become medicine, a physician, and a nurse for them. In order to dispel hunger and thirst during periods of famine, may we become food and drink. To dispel the poverty of sentient beings, may we become an inexhaustible treasure. May we be present before them in the form of countless articles fulfilling their needs. Likewise, in order to serve the purposes of countless sentient beings, from the depths of our heart we offer our physical body, our possessions, and our virtues accumulated in the past, present, and future.

Such offerings are very important, because if we give up everything and make offerings of it, our minds will be able to transcend suffering. Even if we cling to our possessions and material facilities, unwilling to give them up, sooner or later we will have to let them go. Therefore, it is better to offer them to sentient beings while we can, because then we will be able to reap the fruit of doing so for countless lives to come. Therefore, make a dedication from the depths of your heart, offering your physical body to sentient beings so that they can use it and enjoy it as they please.

After these preparatory practices, the actual meditation can begin. If you slightly raise the back of the meditation seat, it will help your meditation. It will help straighten your back, which assists the proper flow of energies within the energy channels. At the outset you must examine your motivation. If your motivation is neutral, immediately try to transform it into a virtuous state of mind. If your mind is under some negative influence, first try to meditate on the flow of your breath. In that way try to remove your negative state of mind and transform it into a neutral state. Then transform that mind into a positive state. This is like dying cloth. White cloth can be dyed any color, but it is difficult to dye cloth that has already been dyed another color. When the mind is overwhelmed by anger or attachment, even if you force yourself to do certain virtuous practices it will be very difficult. So first try to transform your mind into a neutral state through the help of breathing meditation.

During the actual practice recall the subject of your meditation. As you begin each new day, you should generate a strong motivation, thinking, "From now until I die I will try my best to be useful, to be beneficial to other people. At least I will not harm them. I will try to do that until I die, and at least that is what I will do today." Then before you close your eyes at night, you should think back on how you spent your day. If you find that your conduct was useful and beneficial, you can rejoice and make a further determination to spend the rest of your life this way. If you find that you behaved negatively, that you bullied someone or said something nasty or harmful, you must openly admit it. Recollect the kindness of the Buddhas and bodhisattvas and confess your mistake and make a determination not to do the same again. This is the real way to practice the Dharma. If you do not pay attention to this kind of practice, but simply go on leading the same old way of life, you will make no progress. However much time you spend meditating, you should spend it thoughtfully.

Cultivate a thought that even if sentient beings take your life, defame you, or scold you, may they do as they please. If someone wants to play with you, bully you, ignore you, tease you, or make your body an object of amusement or ridicule, offer your body so that they may use it as they please. Then think, "Because I have given this body to all sentient beings from the depth of my heart, they can use it and enjoy it as they please. There is no need for me to protect this body. Let it do whatever does no harm to other sentient beings. Whenever sentient beings focus on me, may they never have to turn away without achieving their purpose. If in connection with me, someone develops anger or feels uneasy, may even that become a cause for their fulfilling their purpose. If anyone addresses me sarcastically, harms me, or mocks me, may they all be able to attain Buddhahood." Whether sentient beings are critical, sarcastic, or mocking, they are making a karmic connection with us. Therefore we wish that this karmic connection may become a cause for their attaining enlightenment.

Right now we are just ordinary people, but we make a wish from the depths of our hearts, that through repeated cultivation of the awakening mind, through repeated commitment and determination, we will attain Buddhahood for the sake of sentient beings. Therefore, the bodhisattva says, "May I in all times, temporarily and ultimately, become a protector for those who are without protection. May I become a guide for those who have lost their path, may I become a ship for those who want to cross huge oceans. May I become a bridge for those who want to cross rivers. May I become an island for those who are troubled or in danger at sea. May I become a lamp for those who need light. May I become a place of habituation for those who are looking for shelter. May I become a servant for those who need one. In other words, may I become all those articles that sentient beings need, whatever form they may take, such as a precious wish-fulfilling jewel, a wish-fulfilling vase, efficacious mantras, medicines, a wish-fulfilling celestial tree, the wish-fulfilling cow. Just like the great elements earth, water, fire, and air and the space on which they depend, may I become an object of enjoyment for infinite sentient beings. May I become the basis for the survival of all sentient beings."

When you are able to cultivate such a mental attitude, there is nothing for you to hang onto or clutch to yourself. You give no opening to your self-centered attitude. You come to a determination that your only purpose is to fulfill the needs of infinite suffering sentient beings.

Just as the great elements have existed forever for the use and service of sentient beings, you make a wish that you likewise may be able to serve all sentient beings.

The bodhisattva further wishes, "May my body, speech, and mind be enjoyed by sentient beings. And may I also take on the experience of all the sufferings of sentient beings, the misdeeds that lead to them, and the disturbing emotions motivating these misdeeds, and may all my pleasant experiences and virtuous qualities be experienced by sentient beings." The bodhisattva concludes, "May I live as long as space endures and may I be able to remove the infinite sufferings of sentient beings."

Such determination is inconceivably marvelous, but this does not mean that we cannot generate it. Through repeated practice we too can generate such a mind. Our present coarse and ignorant mind, if trained and tamed, can gradually be transformed into the awakening mind. "Therefore in all ways and at all times may I become a source of livelihood, a source of enjoyment for all sentient beings, whose number is as limitless as space. And may I be able to serve them until they transcend suffering, until they attain nirvana." This kind of teaching really strengthens your determination.

Here we see ourselves as inferior to other sentient beings. Tiny insects may be helpless, they may be weak, but they are not destructive. They do not harm other beings, they do not disturb other beings' peace. We call ourselves human beings and think of ourselves as very intelligent, but how do we use our intelligence? We deceive other people, seize every opportunity to bully and cheat them. When we compare ourselves to other sentient beings we must try to appreciate their positive qualities. And when we look at ourselves we should try to recognize our faults and reduce them.

The human mind is flexible in many ways. It can take a positive or negative attitude depending on what is required by conditions. From one angle, whenever there is a risk of disturbing emotions arising, we should try to see ourselves as inferior to even the tiniest insects. But from another point of view, when it comes to accomplishing a major task, such as fulfilling the wishes of sentient beings, we should not be despondent. That is when we have to generate mental courage and determination within ourselves. We have to step forward and say, "I alone will take responsibility for serving countless sentient beings." That is what we do when we generate the awakening mind. We visualize Buddhas and bodhisattvas in front of us and make a determination to become a source of peace, happiness, enjoyment, and livelihood for all sentient beings.

Having received such an awakening mind, we should rejoice. We have made our lives meaningful and fruitful, because cultivating the awakening mind lays the foundation for the attainment of Buddhahood. On the one hand we have found this wonderful life as a free and fortunate human being, and on the other we have today been born into the family and lineage of the Buddha. Because we have generated the awakening mind, we have become children of the Buddha. This epithet can sometimes refer only to those who have actually cultivated the awakening mind. We can at least cultivate a semblance of the awakening mind; we are going some way toward it, and this is grounds for rejoicing.

When you embark on such a training, you should do so willingly, voluntarily, and with great joy. If a blind person were somehow to find a rare and precious jewel in a heap of dust, he or she would cherish it and keep it safe. Likewise, even though we are afflicted with disturbing emotions and so forth, because of the teachings of the Great Vehicle and the kindness of our teachers, we have gained some appreciation for the awakening mind. And because of this we have been able to cultivate the awakening mind today. This precious mind is the supreme elixir for overcoming death, because it leads to the attainment of Buddhahood.

In the short run, if you simply have a mind that wishes to benefit other sentient beings, you will have more courage, your mind will be more relaxed, and the elements of your body will be more in balance. If you take medicine you will more easily digest it. Even a small amount of altruism is like the supreme elixir that overcomes death and its causes. The awakening mind is also like an inexhaustible treasure dispelling the poverty of sentient beings. In the short run it removes poverty when you are within the cycle of existence. Ultimately, all the excellent qualities within the cycle of existence, the state of liberation, and Buddhahood are the result of the awakening mind. It is also like a supreme medicine healing a sentient beings' sickness. It is like a wish-fulfilling tree in whose shade exhausted wandering beings can rest and relax. It is like a bridge over which sentient beings can be liberated from their negative states of existence.

Cultivating the awakening mind is like the moon shining, dispelling the darkness of disturbing emotions. It is like the bright sun removing the murky ignorance of sentient beings. It is like the butter obtained by churning the milk of the Dharma. Sentient beings are like travelers wandering endlessly on the paths of the cycle of existence. This mind wishing to benefit other sentient beings is like the very sustenance of these wandering sentient beings. All of us wandering in the cycle of existence are the same. The only difference is that today, because of our merit, because of the kindness of our teachers, and because we have encountered the Buddha's teachings, we are able to cultivate such an awakening mind in the presence of the Buddhas and bodhisattvas.

CHAPTER 4

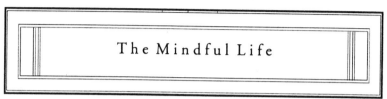

The Mindful Life

I have found the path of cultivating the awakening mind to be the source of all happiness. It is the way to fulfill our own purpose and the purposes of other sentient beings. How could we give it up?

Those of us who try to follow the bodhisattva's way of life have taken on a great responsibility, providing the ultimate welfare of all beings in the universe. It is important that we study the different bodhisattva precepts outlining how we should train and the various faults to avoid. Recollecting these practices is not enough, we should ensure that in our actual lives we do not behave negatively in body, speech, or mind. We must restrain ourselves from engaging in wrong deeds. We should develop this practice to the point that even in dreams we are mindful. If we can do that we will be able to preserve our awakening mind without letting it degenerate.

If, even for a moment, you obstruct other sentient beings from accumulating merit, if you hinder, even for a moment, the development of the awakening mind, you are hindering the bodhisattva who is fulfilling the purposes of countless sentient beings. As a result, in the future you will have to spend infinite lives in unfavorable states of existence. If destroying the peace and happiness of one sentient being can cause you to fall from your well-placed rebirth, what will be the result of destroying the peace and happiness of sentient beings whose number is equal to the extent of space? Consequently, if you sometimes cultivate a powerful awakening mind but sometimes also commit serious infractions, if you sometimes let your mind degenerate and you sometimes strengthen and cultivate the awakening mind, if you mix them both in your daily life, it will take a long time to attain the higher levels of spiritual development. Therefore, making a strong commitment with confidence and courage, you must fulfill the trainings of a bodhisattva.

You must reflect that if you do not strive in the training and practice of a bodhisattva you will tumble from one unfavorable birth to another. If, because of disturbing emotions and negative attitudes, you fall into an unfavorable state of existence, the Buddhas will be unable to help you. Countless compassionate Buddhas have appeared and worked for the benefit of sentient beings. But because of your own faults you did not become an object of their care. If you remain careless and let your mind be invaded by disturbing emotions, you will fall again and again into unfavorable states of existence where even the Buddhas will be unable to help you. Even if you free yourself from unfavorable states of existence, you will be subject to sickness, injury, and other constraints. Therefore, it is important that you personally engage in the accumulation of virtuous qualities and the elimination of unwholesome activities.

Today we have a very precious opportunity. We are human, the teaching of the Buddha exists, we have faith and the opportunity to develop virtuous qualities. Such circumstances are rare. We may be healthy right now. We may possess an abundance of material goods and we may be free from harm. But the nature of life is deceptive; it passes away moment by moment. Our physical body is like something we have borrowed. At present we are preoccupied by disturbing emotions and engage in negative activities. Because of these we will definitely be unable to attain even the life of a human being in the future. And if we do not obtain a human life, but fall into an unfavorable state of existence, we will continue to accumulate only negative deeds. We will be unable to do anything virtuous. Occasionally we may have a chance to do something wholesome, but we will have to make a special effort. Otherwise we will fall into more unfavorable states of existence. We will experience great suffering, and our minds will be confused and overwhelmingly ignorant. Under such circumstances we will have no opportunity to do anything virtuous. Unable to do anything virtuous, having accumulated great negativity and having fallen into unfavorable states of existence for hundreds and hundreds of eons, we may not even hear the words "happy existence," let alone find a well-placed rebirth.

It is because of this that the compassionate Buddha Shakyamuni taught the following allegory. Imagine a huge ocean on the surface of which floats a yoke with a hole through the middle. In the depths of that ocean there lives a blind tortoise who comes to the surface once in a hundred years. The chances of finding a human life again in the future are similar to the chances of the turtle surfacing with its head through the hole in the yoke afloat on the huge ocean. Such is the rarity and difficulty of finding a human life. We have accumulated countless negative deeds. And yet, as a result of one negative deed lasting for one moment, we may find ourselves living in hell undergoing ceaseless suffering. If that happens we will definitely not be able to achieve birth in a happy existence.

It is also not the case that once we have experienced the results of our negative deeds we will be free from them. While experiencing the results of one set of negative deeds, we find ourselves in a negative state of existence, and because of the disturbing emotions existing within our minds, we continue to accumulate negative deeds, which in turn create more suffering. We have a strong predisposition within our minds, which circumstances tend to reinforce, to activate negative attitudes and disturbing emotions. Once we fall into an unfavorable state of existence, it will be very difficult to free ourselves from it. So, having found life as a free and fortunate human being, if we do not make ourselves familiar with virtuous qualities, if we do not cultivate a spiritual path, it is like intentionally deceiving ourselves.

We want happiness; we do not want suffering. We have the opportunity to cultivate the causes of happiness and remove the causes of suffering. If we pass up such an opportunity and take no positive steps, what could be more foolish? As the result of accumulating negative deeds, when we come to die we will have dreadful visions of hell; we will die in great fear and anguish. After a brief stay in the intermediate state of existence, we will be born in an unfavorable state. We may find ourselves living in hell. Pained and tormented, we will be filled with remorse. Our minds will be engulfed by suffering. We have found a rare and favorable state, whether by chance or coincidence. We can acknowledge this and discriminate between what is good temporarily and what is good in the long run. If we nevertheless do not start spiritual practice but let ourselves be led into a worse state of existence, it will be as if our minds had fallen under a spell. We will be like people without minds.

Disturbing emotions abide peacefully within our minds, harming and destroying us. Consider the destructiveness of disturbing emotions. When anger arises within us, it may seem as if a good friend had come to our aid. It is almost as if anger said, "Don't worry, I am here, I'll help you." You might have been about to run from your opponent, but as soon as anger arises it lends you a kind of false courage. It makes you feel bolder and you foolishly retaliate. Attachment comes to us as a soft-spoken friend. It deceives us and gradually destroys us. Because of strong attachment and anger we lose our discriminative awareness. When you are angry it is as if you have gone completely mad. Because of this madness you lose your sense of discrimination. You might strike out at you opponent and accidentally hit someone else. Likewise, when you speak to other people out of anger, you may say unreasonable and provocative things that should not be said. Once our attachment has subsided we realize our errors and are filled with remorse. But by then the deed has been done.

Normally, we think of enemies as something external. We think of evil spirits and hostile forces existing somewhere else. We point at enemies existing outside ourselves and look to other external forces to protect ourselves from them. But according to the teachings of the Buddha, external enemies are not our real enemies. Such external forces may be temporarily hostile, but they can gradually be turned into friends. Besides, even these so-called enemies are like ourselves in wanting happiness and not wanting suffering. These so-called enemies are actually suitable objects for our compassion.

If we think of enemies as those who bring us even short-lived harm, then even our own physical bodies are our enemies, because they are the basis for much of our pain. Likewise, we should see our minds as our enemies, because when we are despondent we feel altogether unhappy. Our external enemies could be our enemies today but our friends tomorrow. We cannot count on their remaining implacable foes.

The real enemies are our disturbing emotions. They are our true enemies right from the start and will remain so forever. What is an enemy? An enemy is someone who brings us harm. In the Buddhist scriptures, disturbing emotions are identified as our enemy. To attain liberation or nirvana is to achieve victory over our enemy, the disturbing emotions. Attaining nirvana does not mean changing our physical body or moving to another planet. Among Tibetans, ordinary people referring to family life often say, "Now I am wandering in the cycle of existence." According to them, if you have no family problems you are apparently liberated. But that is not the real meaning of liberation. Our physical body itself is a kind of cycle of existence, because it is on the basis of this physical existence that we accumulate negative activities. Attachment, craving, and hatred have been identified as enemies residing within ourselves. Although they lack weapons, we are enslaved and rendered helpless by them. Their influence and effect are terribly destructive.

If we cannot fight, we can run away from our external enemies. For example, in 1959, when we were surrounded by Chinese troops, we somehow escaped across the mountains. In the past, people used to hide in impregnable forts. Nowadays, of course, if you were to stay in a fort you would only become a target. In the past, kings used to live in forts under the impression that they could live there forever. That is why we see many forts still standing in India. Similarly, the Great Wall of China, constructed at great cost in terms of human labor, was built with the same motivation. But if, even after so much construction, the enemy still resides within you, there is nothing you can do. How can you hide from that? There may be some harmful entities like bacteria residing within us that can be destroyed by taking medicine or having an injection. But we cannot rely on any external force to destroy and eliminate the disturbing emotions. They are the real enemy.

Even if all the gods in the universe joined forces against you, if every living being became hostile toward you, they would not have the power to send you to hell. Disturbing emotions, on the other hand, can deliver you to hell in a single instant. This is why disturbing emotions have been our enemy from beginningless time, harming and destroying us. There has never been an enemy so enduring as these disturbing emotions. Ordinary enemies die and disappear. If you comply with the wishes of an ordinary enemy, gradually he or she will become your friend. Your enemy will become someone who brings you benefit. In the case of disturbing emotions, the more you rely on them, the more they will harm you and bring suffering to you. They have been our constant enemy of long duration, the sole cause of all our sufferings. As long as we let this enemy reside peacefully within us, we will have no happiness.

If you let yourself become entangled in the net of attachment, how can you expect to find happiness? You must identify the disturbing emotions as your real enemy. Having identified them, you must employ antidotes and generate mental courage to face and resist them. You must understand the disturbing emotions as the source of all sufferings and problems. In ordinary life, when we run up against a minor problem, we tend to get angry and want to retaliate. And when we are unable to overcome the problem we are unable to sleep. When soldiers go to war, they voluntarily undergo the suffering of being wounded and do not return home until the war is won, displaying their scars proudly. Then why should we not be proud to undergo such hardships when we are involved in the positive task of fighting the disturbing emotions? To obtain relatively minor benefits in the course of their work, fishermen, butchers, and farmers will put up with many temporary hardships. Why then can we not put up with the various hardships and problems associated with the more important task of achieving Buddhahood for the sake of all sentient beings?

When you wage a war with an ordinary enemy you might gain the victory and drive the enemy from your country. Ordinary enemies can regroup, reinforce, and reequip themselves and return to the battle. But when you fight the disturbing emotions, once you have defeated and eliminated them, they cannot return. From this perspective disturbing emotions are weak; we do not need nuclear missiles or bombs to destroy them. They are weak because once we are able to see reality and cultivate the eye of wisdom, we can remove the disturbing emotions. And once we destroy the disturbing emotions within our minds, where will they go? They disappear into emptiness. They cannot retreat somewhere else and reinforce themselves, so they cannot return to harm us.

There is no disturbing emotion that has independent existence. When attachment and anger arise within our minds, they are quite powerful and leave our minds disturbed. Even so, on closer scrutiny they have no special place to hide. They do not abide in the body, nor do they abide in our sense faculties. If you try to find disturbing emotions among the collection of mental and physical components or outside them, you will not find them there. Disturbing emotions are like an illusion. Why should we let them plunge us into hell?

If you always remain careful and alert, you will know what is to be practiced and what is to be given up. Having identified what is worth doing and what is not, if you are conscientious you will notice when you are beginning to behave negatively. Then you can restrain yourself. Care and attention are very important, and how closely you pay attention depends upon the strength of your mindfulness. The best means for sustaining attention is to examine your physical, verbal, and mental behavior and to remain watchful all the time. The mind is like an elephant: if you let it wonder around without any control, it will wreak havoc. But the harm and suffering you will encounter as a result of not guarding your mind far exceed the damage done by a rampaging wild elephant.

The question is how to discipline the mind. You need mindfulness, which is like a rope in all your activities, whether they be physical, mental, or verbal. With the rope of mindfulness tie the elephantlike mind to the pillar of the object of your meditation. In other words, tie your mind to virtuous qualities and do not let it wander toward unwholesome topics. Pay attention to the direction the mind is going in. If you find your mind moving in a positive direction, you should rejoice and strengthen it. If you are able to keep your mind on a positive track, you will be able to overcome all fears.

Both positive and negative experiences arise from the mind, depending on whether your mind is transformed or not. Therefore, it is most important to control and discipline the mind. All the fears and the immeasurable sufferings that we encounter arise from the mind. The Buddha taught that there is no enemy that is more powerful than the mind. In all the realms of existence there is nothing more frightful, more to be feared, than the mind. Likewise, he said that the disciplined mind gives rise to all excellent qualities. The source and cause of peace and happiness is the mind. Happiness arises from virtuous practice, sufferings arise from negative practice. So happiness and suffering depend upon whether your mind is transformed or not. Even in the short term, the more you control and discipline your mind, the happier and more relaxed you will be.

Once the mind within is controlled and relaxed, even if the whole universe appears to turn on you like an enemy, you will not feel threatened or unhappy. On the other hand, if you are internally disturbed and agitated, even if the most delicious food is laid out on the table in front of you, you will not enjoy it. You may hear pleasant things, but they will bring you no joy. So depending on whether you mind is disciplined or not, you will experience happiness or suffering.

Once you transform your mind so that you have no possessiveness and no craving, you will achieve the perfection of giving. The perfection of giving means that you offer everything that you have, as well as the positive results of that offering, to all sentient beings. The practice is entirely dependent on the mind. The perfection of ethics is similar. Achieving the perfection of ethics means that you attain a state of mind that refrains from harming sentient beings in any way at all. It is a state completely free from self-centeredness. The practice of patience is the same. Unruly sentient beings are as infinite as the extent of space. However, once you control your own mind, it is as if you had destroyed all external enemies. If your mind is calm, even though the whole environment is hostile, you will not be disturbed. To protect your feet from thorns, you cannot cover the entire surface of the earth with leather. A more effective method is to cover the soles of your feet with leather.

If you want to protect the mind, you must make an effort to maintain mindfulness. When you do not pay attention and your mindfulness degenerates, the merit you accumulated in the past will be lost as if it had been stolen by thieves. Consequently, you will fall into an unfavorable state of existence. The disturbing emotions are like robbers and thieves. They are always alert, looking for an opportunity. If they find it, they take it and rob you of virtue. They take the life of our happy existence. Therefore, never allow your mindfulness to weaken. If you occasionally lose your mindfulness, restore it by remembering the endless sufferings in the cycle of existence.

What are the methods for maintaining mindfulness and alertness? To associate with spiritual teachers and to listen to teachings, to know what is to be practiced and what is to be given up. The more respect you have for the teachings, the more careful you will be. When you associate with good friends, you will remain naturally alert. You can discover what is to be given up and what is to be practiced by listening to teachings and following the example of good friends. When you reflect on explanations of the nature of impermanence and the sufferings of the cycle of existence, you will cultivate fear within your mind. Because of such fear, a fortunate person will quickly be able to be mindful.

The other method for cultivating mindfulness is to remember that Buddhas and bodhisattvas possess an omniscient mind. They constantly know what you are doing. When you remember their presence you will be more careful. You will be ashamed if you do something negative. Since the Buddhas and bodhisattvas possess unobstructed awareness, we cannot hide anything from them. Understanding this and remaining respectful is the practice of recollecting the Buddhas. Normally, we tend to think that the Buddhas and bodhisattvas will pay attention to us only if we recite some prayer or invocation, or call them by name. This is a mistake. The Buddha's omniscient mind pervades everything, even the subtlest particles. In other words, the Buddha's mind is aware of all phenomena, regardless of time and place. Understanding that you are always in the presence of the omniscient Buddhas is the way to recollect the Buddha and his qualities. This is very important for your daily practice.

If you are mindful, when one of these defects is about to arise you will be able to restrain yourself. For example, it may be that while you are talking to someone else you begin to get angry. Your mindfulness will prompt you either to stop the conversation or to change the subject. Think to yourself that even though the other person is being unreasonable and using provocative words, there is no use in retaliating in kind. Instead of dwelling on this situation, turn your mind to the other person's good points. This will also help reduce your anger.

The elephantlike mind is intoxicated by the disturbing emotions, so you should bind it to the great pillar of spiritual practice. With all your effort examine your mind, and try not to let it wander even for a moment. Watch what it is about to do and what it is doing. When you are about to meditate, for example, at the outset you must cultivate an intention to be careful and not to let yourself be distracted. As a result, you may be successful in meditating for about fifteen minutes without being distracted. Once you get used to it, you can lengthen the session.

Of course, it is difficult to control the mind and make it stay on the object of meditation. It is difficult to make your mind do what you want it to, but as you gradually get used to it you will achieve some success. You can employ whatever techniques help you control your mind. For example, you might find that sitting facing a wall helps you to control your distractions when you are doing certain meditations. Sometimes closing your eyes may help. At other times keeping them open may be of more help. It depends on your personal inclination and your circumstances.

This is how to always be alert and guard against the disturbing emotions and against getting involved in meaningless activity. If you want to go somewhere or you want to say something, first determine whether it is proper or not. When attachment is about to rise within you, or you feel like getting angry with someone, do not do anything, do not speak, do not think—remain like a piece of wood. If you find yourself inclined to break into meaningless laughter, or you want to brag about something, or you want to discuss the faults of others, or you want to deceive others, or you want to say something improper or to make sarcastic remarks, or you want to praise yourself and criticize or scold others, at that time remain like a piece of wood. If you find you want to obtain possessions, respect, fame, and renown or you want to gather a coterie of followers around you, remain like a piece of wood. If you find that you are inclined to neglect the purposes of others but aspire to fulfill your own purpose and, what is more, you want to talk about it, remain like a piece of wood. When you are inclined to become impatient, lazy, or despondent, or you want to make presumptuous remarks, or you are inclined to become self-satisfied, remain like a piece of wood.

Immature people are those who have little mental or spiritual growth. Such narrow-minded people are like squabbling children who are unable to live together. Do not be discouraged by their lack of contentment. Instead, generate compassion for them, reflecting that the disgruntled expressions of these children are due to the preponderance of disturbing emotions in their minds. This accounts for their frivolous behavior. Do not follow their example. Through meditation on wisdom you should be able to see yourself as free from an intrinsically existent self. Regard yourself as an emanation of the bodhisattvas. Constantly retain this in your mind and determine ultimately to fulfill the purpose of this precious human life.

It is also important to counter our attachment to our physical body. At the time of death our body may be dragged about by vultures, but we will not care. Why then are we so attached to this body now? If we borrow something from a very powerful person, we remember that sooner or later we will have to return it. Our present body is like something we have borrowed. However much we try to guard it, sooner or later we have to leave it behind. What is the use of having so much attachment to and spending so much effort on the physical body? Sooner or later we have to leave it behind and, in the meantime, it provokes so much unnecessary behavior that is the source of so much trouble.

Let us see what we mean when we describe the body as unpleasant. First let us think about our skin. On the surface it seems to be pleasant and pink. Mentally examine it. Think about what is just beneath the skin: mounds of flesh joined by tendons, sinews, nerve channels, and so forth. We have all seen illustrations of the human brain and X rays that reveal the skeleton. This is the reality: a collection of bones covered with flesh and skin. But we think, "This is my beautiful, handsome body." In your mind, examine all this in detail. Look and see what is hidden beneath the flesh. Under the flesh is a frame of bones, and if you split the bones, you will find blood and marrow and so forth. What essence is there? Why should we cherish it so much? We feel we have to take such care of our bodies. We need clothes and food. Not just any clothes, but the most beautiful clothes. Of course there is a reason to protect ourselves from cold and heat, but why should we spend so much money and use so much costly cloth just to cover our bodies? In addition, wealthier people feel they need ornaments. They make holes in their ears and fix earrings through them. Others pierce their noses and put rings there too.

All these activities are the results of mental confusion, total ignorance. What is the point? You should explore the matter yourself, but you will never be able to find any essence in the body. It is human intelligence that makes so many things up, that creates so many different categories. We strengthen the disturbing emotions, saying that these people are rich, these people are beautiful. To some extent it is understandable for lay people to behave like this, but when those who are ordained wear ornamental clothes it is a disgrace. Think of how the Buddha lived. He was a very simple monk without any ornaments.

So, if you examine your body, you will find it has no essence; it is just a collection of extremely unpleasant substances; it is like a machine for producing filthy substances. Why then do you still generate so much attachment to it? Why do you guard this physical body? You cannot eat these unpleasant substances, you cannot drink this blood, you cannot gnaw the intestines. What is the use of this body? Are we protecting this body so that at the time of death we will be able to offer it to the vultures? The original substances from which our bodies grow are the ovum and semen from our parents. But if you were to come across a puddle of these substances on the floor, you would be utterly disgusted. If you trace it back, your body is the result of the essence of countless generations of such unpleasant substances. Similarly, if you closely examine the nature of the physical body itself, the flesh, blood, and bones by themselves are all repulsive.

Every day until we die, we eat and drink to sustain our body. I have already passed sixty years of age. Over these sixty years of my life how much food have I eaten, how much meat have I consumed? How many lives has my life cost? We make such an effort to sustain our bodies. If we do so to little purpose it would perhaps have been better to have been born as an animal or an insect. Then at least we would do less harm to other sentient beings.

If we are unable to use our human intelligence in a positive way, there is no purpose to human life. We will simply be machines to produce manure. Human beings should be able to use their intelligence, their discriminating awareness, to contribute to the welfare of all sentient beings. That is how to make life meaningful. That is the way to bring about peace, both temporarily and in the long run. There is nothing amazing about being highly educated; there is nothing amazing about being rich. If we have no compassion or feeling for other sentient beings, whatever material facilities or education we may have will be of no meaning and of no use. Therefore, we should use our human body to preserve our human intelligence in order to be able to engage in virtuous practice.

Try to gain control of yourself and realize that helping other sentient beings is the purpose of life. If you are able to understand that, you will always be able to gain control over your mind and body and use them for the sake of other sentient beings. Human beings have the intelligence to cultivate the awakening mind, to exchange their own welfare for the sufferings of other sentient beings, by which means they can achieve Buddhahood. This is how to gain freedom, to become independent. With assurance, with courage, and with the confidence of achieving the ultimate goal, meet other people with a smile and stop scowling at them. Welcome everyone with compassion, straightforwardly, with a feeling of affection. Treat all sentient beings as your friends.

Do not behave in a way that might disturb or harm other people. Conduct yourself calmly and humbly. Be like a cat who goes about its business quietly and stealthily, without much ado. When someone says something beneficial or gives you unsought advice, accept it with respect. Accept other people's good qualities and see yourself as a student of all sentient beings. Whenever someone says something positive and worthwhile, commend it. If you see someone doing something virtuous, offer your praise. You can praise people to their faces, but it can seem like flattery; it is better to praise them to others. When someone praises someone else, join in applauding that person's qualities. In such circumstances we are often inclined to be skeptical, saying, "Yes, but..." or even denying the person's qualities and reciting his or her faults. If someone else comments on your own good qualities, examine whether you have such a quality or not. Do not let yourself get puffed up, thinking you are something special. Instead of becoming proud, just appreciate that good qualities have been acknowledged.

When I was a child, my late abbot taught me the art of writing. He told me the story of a lama giving a teaching. It seems that he said that baldness, a goiter, and a beard are the only ornaments of an ordained person. Among his listeners was a monk who possessed all these features. He felt pleased to possess these ornaments and started to stretch out his neck with pride. But when the lama went on to say that if one monk were to possess all three features, it would be a bad omen, he drew his neck back in a hurry. The point is that if someone praises your qualities, you should not get puffed up. Simply think that the person is good because he or she recognizes good qualities.

Whatever project you start should contribute to making sentient beings happy. Pleasure and happiness of the mind cannot be bought. They can only be cultivated within the mind. If someone is happy, simply enjoy their happiness. Be happy that others are happy. Without competitiveness or feelings of jealousy, try to benefit other people. If you do so, you will naturally find satisfaction. You will have the contentment of having made your life meaningful. You can be confident that you never bear enmity toward other people, and you never disturb them.

People who constantly affront and disturb others always feel disturbed themselves, not only when they are awake but even in their dreams. If you help other people and create a climate of peace and happiness, you will enjoy peace and happiness yourself, even in your dreams. The happiness obtained from seeing other people happy is pure and uncontaminated happiness. It is real profit, now and in the future. However, if you feel unhappy and jealous when others are happy, you are likely to suffer sore eyes, pains in your back, and high blood pressure. Here and now you will be miserable and physically uncomfortable, and in your future life there will be great suffering.

How should you look upon other sentient beings? Whenever you see other beings before you, think that by depending on these sentient beings you will attain Buddhahood. In this way remember their kindness, and view them with love. If you help and support those who possess good qualities, those who have been kind to you, or those who are suffering, you will accumulate great merit. For example, show respect to your seniors, such as your parents and other old people. The elderly should accept the good and creative qualities of youth. And youth should show respect and try to learn from the experience of the elderly. Harmonious relations between parents and children are particularly important. It is the parents' duty to take care of their children, and if they do, their children will respond with gratitude. In many countries, nowadays, parents and children are not very close. Parents have little affection for their children, and their children show them little respect. As such children grow up, they hope that their old parents will soon die. Parents too prefer to live away from their children.

It is important to help the helpless and downtrodden. When we see someone well-dressed and attractive, we feel inclined to offer our help immediately, but when we see someone dressed in ragged clothes, looking unwell, we try to turn away. This is not a good sign. The attractive and well-dressed may be deceptive, whereas the helpless actually pose no threat. When I see a beggar, I try never to think of him or her as somehow inferior to or weaker than me. I never think that I am better than a beggar. But when I meet people who pretend to be intelligent and clever, I tend not to give in to them immediately. If someone is straightforward and pleasant, we can be too. If you meet people open-heartedly and receive a similar response, you can soon become friends. But if you remain honest and open and the other person reacts in the opposite way, then of course you have to adopt another ploy in response. Whatever you do, it is important not to bully or deceive those who are already downtrodden.

Remain alert and become skillful in what is to be practiced and what is to be given up. Have the confidence to engage in positive activities without simply depending on other people for their support. Do not give up a major practice for the sake of a minor practice. The most important thing is that whatever you do should benefit other people; it should have the effect of fulfilling the wishes of other people. Having understood this crucial point, we should make constant efforts on behalf of other people. This is what the compassionate Buddha has taught. The Buddha was farsighted and knew what would be useful in the long term and what would be useful in the short term. This is why his advice is flexible and why a bodhisattva who constantly works for the benefit of others is sometimes permitted to do things that are normally prohibited.

We should share our food with three kinds of beings: those who have fallen into unfavorable states of existence, like hungry spirits; those who are without protection, like beggars and animals; and those observing the practice of morality, which refers to ordained people such as monks and nuns. Dividing our food into four parts, we should give away three parts and take one. Whenever you eat or drink something, make offerings to the Buddha, Dharma, and Sangha, give some of it to beggars, and dedicate some of it to hungry spirits.

Your body is the basis on which you observe your spiritual practice, so you should not sacrifice it lightly. You should avoid the two extremes. Do not lead too luxurious a life, wearing all kinds of ornaments and exotic clothes, eating too much rich food, because doing so is a way of exhausting your merit. But also do not fall to the other extreme of asceticism that leads to total exhaustion. Such mortification as going about naked in all kinds of weather or piercing your limbs with weapons is another extreme. Do not impose hardship on yourself to no purpose. If you make your body inefficient, it will hinder your Dharma practice. However, if you observe the three trainings in ethics, meditation, and wisdom, relying on this very body, you will quickly be able to fulfill the wishes of sentient beings.

It is very dangerous too to adopt sectarian attitudes, because the different levels of the Buddha's teaching are supposed to be for attaining

Buddhahood. If, instead of using them to attain Buddhahood, we use them to create conflict among different schools or different religious traditions, it is very unfortunate. So it is important that we make ourselves thoroughly familiar with all the teachings, without any sectarian bias, through hearing, thinking, and meditation. There are two ways of approaching this. In the past there were scholarly adepts who simply concentrated on understanding their own school and tradition and had nothing to say about other sects or schools. Then there was another category of scholarly adepts who could study the teachings of all traditions. In the present situation in the modern world, the second approach is now more appropriate.

Among western Buddhist practitioners there are many who are familiar only with their own school and do not know anything beyond that. Consequently, they feel apprehensive about the authenticity of other schools and other teachings. In response I try to explain that all four Tibetan Buddhist schools follow the same teaching of the Buddha without any contradiction. From my personal point of view I have found it very useful and beneficial to study and practice teachings found in all four schools. When I explain this, some people reply that they would dearly like to find a teacher who can explain all these schools, but there are very few people who have the knowledge and experience to explain all four schools of Tibetan Buddhism. Still, we should try to understand all the different levels of the four schools and effectively fulfill the wishes of many people.

In Tibet the population is sparse, and the air and water are fresh. Before the Chinese came, all the water was potable. Because of the climate and environment, we did not need to pay special attention to health and sanitation. Nowadays in many developed countries there is so much pollution that people have to take preventive measures to protect their children. We have to educate ourselves about these things. We have the basic qualities already, because we talk about the welfare of all sentient beings. For example, if you were to dig up the ground or cut the grass to no purpose, it would harm or disturb the lives of insects and other animals. Such concern for insects and animals is good reason for preserving the environment. Those who understand it better should come forward and help others to understand the need to preserve the environment.

Of the many practices of a bodhisattva, training the mind is the most important. In practice or in training, bodhisattvas neglect nothing. Therefore, there is nothing that does not help them produce merit. Whether you do so directly or indirectly, concern yourself only with fulfilling the wishes of sentient beings, and dedicate all your virtuous activity to their benefit. Observing the conduct of a bodhisattva means restraining the self-centered attitude. So, influenced by mindfulness and remaining alert, you must engage in genuine practice. What is the use simply of talk? You must actually practice. How could it help a sick person merely to read a medical text? It is not enough simply to discuss the practices of a bodhisattva. We must put them into practice.

CHAPTER 5

Patience

Among all the factors that can help sustain the awakening mind and safeguard this wholesome thought from degeneration, the practice of patience is the most effective. This is because when people attempt to hurt us or inflict harm upon us, there is a great danger of our losing our kind and compassionate attitude. Only the observance of patience can help us.

The first step in this process is to think about the benefits of patience and the dire consequences of anger and hatred. Practicing patience is the most effective way to maintain our peace of mind. Whether we are confronted by adverse circumstances or hostile forces, we will remain undisturbed and our minds will still be clear. In the long term, we will be able to develop courage and strong determination. On the other hand, anger and hostility can cause great damage in this life as well as in future lives. No matter how polite and amiable we normally are, when anger erupts, all our good qualities vanish in seconds. For instance, someone may have been a close friend, but because of something we say or do in anger, we can lose that friendship. Anger disturbs our own peace of mind as well as that of everyone around us. It creates conflict and unhappiness. Anger has the potential to hamper our progress in life. It gives rise to coarse physical and verbal behavior that we would otherwise be too embarrassed to engage in. When we are overcome by anger, we might even go to the extreme of taking someone's life. Such negative actions leave strong imprints on the mind that can result in our taking birth in miserable forms of existence. Whatever virtuous qualities you have accumulated over countless eons by practicing generosity and making offerings to the Buddhas can be destroyed in one instant of anger. This refers particularly to occasions when a person becomes angry with a bodhisattva. No other negative deed compares with anger as an obstacle and hindrance to cultivating the spiritual path. Similarly, there is no penance equal to patience. Therefore, reinforce patience in as many ways as you can.

Anger can have several causes, unhappiness and anxiety among them. We tend to respond to events and circumstances in our lives irrationally. When something is troubling us, we tend to blame other people for the problem. Instead of reacting instantly, we should examine the problem with a cooler head. The first step is to see if there is a solution. If the problem can be solved, there is no need to worry about it. But if the problem cannot be overcome, worrying about it will do no good. By adopting a more rational approach we can prevent events from disturbing our minds. Let us take an example. If someone strikes us with a stick, our usual impulse reaction is to be angry with that person and want revenge. What the Dharma teaches us is that we should calm down and look for the real cause. Now the question is, which is the real cause—the person, his or her deluded mind, or the stick that actually struck us? When we follow this line of reasoning it becomes clear that we should be angry with the disturbing emotion that prompted the person to act violently. This is an example of how we should be more rational in the way we respond to negative events in our lives.

So long as our mind is filled with the pain of anger, we will never experience peace and happiness. As we all know, as soon as anger arises within us it becomes difficult for us to breathe. We feel suffocated. Under such circumstances how can we sleep or enjoy the taste of our food? We will have no mental or physical peace, and without sleep our minds will become unstable. The scriptures explain that the result of generating anger in this life is to be born as an ugly person in the future. Of course there are some cunning people, and I count some of the Tibetan aristocrats among them, who, the angrier they feel inside, the more they outwardly smile. Apart from them, most of us show anger immediately. For example, in Amdo, the region of northeastern Tibet that I come from, the moment the people there become angry their faces turn red. We have a Tibetan saying: "Do not behave like the people from Amdo." Central Tibet is known as the land of the Dharma. Although the people who live there might not have been able to discipline and transform their minds, some have learned to control the expression on their faces, so that they can still smile even when they are angry.

When anger flares up within us we immediately look ugly. Our faces become wrinkled and red. Even animals, like cats, express anger in very ugly ways. When you are aware of the negativity of disturbing emotions and you watch someone get angry, you are able to see the evidence clearly before you. Anger not only makes us ugly to look at, it also makes us stupid and clumsy. It robs us of our sense of discrimination. If someone harms you and you become angry in return, does that compensate for the harm you have undergone? In the short term anger is of no use, and its effect on our future lives will just be to induce further suffering. The alternative, since you have already been harmed, is simply to bear it and meditate on patience. This course is much better, because it will at least stave off some future suffering. If you get angry, then besides the harm you have already suffered, you will experience further suffering in the future. Anger is a factor that is of no use at all. Just put it behind you.

Although the tantric texts speak of "using hatred in the path," the connotation of the word "anger" in this case is different. We cannot use ordinary hatred on the spiritual path, because such hatred eliminates our compassion and makes our mind rough and wild. Because of anger, we might take the lives even of those who have given us material help, who have shown us kindness and respect. Because of anger we disappoint our friends and turn down gifts. In short, anger never brings peace and happiness. No one is peaceful and happy when they are angry. Anger is an enemy that brings forth negative results.

After you have thought about the advantages of patience and the disadvantages of anger, you should try to understand the causes that give rise to anger. Then you can begin to overcome anger by eliminating its causes. What fuels anger is frustration when we do not achieve what we want or when we experience what we do not want. Anger arises with all its destructive ramifications. The fuel that feeds anger is mental distress, and this is what we must try to prevent. Ordinary enemies may do us harm, but they do other things as well. Even our enemy has to sleep, eat, and look after his family and friends. Ordinary enemies cannot make a continuous and concerted effort to disturb and destroy other people's minds. Anger, however, only and always disturbs the mind. Its only function is to do us harm. Therefore, whatever the cost, we should prevent anger from ever arising by not fueling it with mental distress.

Remaining upset does not fulfill our wishes or bring us happiness and peace. It is disturbing and disruptive. If you feel something unpleasant is about to happen to you, but it is possible to avert it, there is no need to be upset about it; simply do what must be done to avert it. But if nothing can be done, again there is no point in getting upset. Feeling upset will not help. Anxiety and worry solve no problems. If the causes and conditions have come together, we cannot stop them coming to fruition. This is the law of nature. When your predicament cannot be changed, you will only make it worse if you give in to fear, anxiety, and worry. When two people are afflicted by the same kind of sickness, but one is also subject to great anxiety while the other is not, it is quite clear which of them is worse off.

If you compare Tibetan refugees with those from other countries, you will find that the Tibetan attitude is generally courageous. Tibetans do not get too excited or too depressed; despite the depth of suffering they have had to face, they have been able to bear it. Some have encountered intolerable suffering. They have spent up to twenty years in prison, and yet some of them have told me that it was the best time of their lives, because they were able to do intense prayer, meditation, and virtuous practice. Here is the difference in mental attitude. Most people faced with such suffering day and night would lack the fortitude to bear it. But if you can accept the opportunity and use it for transforming the mind, some good can come of it. Therefore, if something can be changed or transformed, there is no need to worry. And if it cannot be changed, there is also no need to worry, because worrying will not solve the problem.

As spiritual practitioners our attitude should be that we will voluntarily undergo hardship in our pursuit of a higher purpose. Faced with minor worldly problems and sufferings, we should be able to adopt a broad-minded attitude so that they will not bother us. If we are able to transform our attitude toward different levels of suffering, it will change our lives. Reflecting on suffering actually has positive results; without it we are unable to generate a determination to be free of this cycle of existence. Therefore, with a firm mind we should reflect on the nature of suffering. There are people who mortify and mutilate themselves under the guise of religion. If people are prepared to undergo hardship for such meaningless purposes, why can't we undergo certain hardships to attain the state of liberation, an enduring state of peace and happiness? Why do we flinch from hardship for the sake of liberation?

It is the nature of the mind that the better acquainted it becomes with doing something, the easier that thing is to do. If we are able to view suffering from a transformed perspective, we will be able to tolerate even greater levels of suffering. There is nothing that does not become easier with familiarity. If we get used to putting up with minor hurts, we will gradually develop tolerance for greater pain. We see many people who put up with being attacked by insects, with the discomfort of hunger and thirst, with being pricked and scratched by thorns as they go about their way of life. People face all such meaningless sufferings easily once they get used to them. Therefore, when we encounter minor problems due to heat and cold, wind and rain, sickness and injury, to fret will only make the problem worse. Some people, instead of being frightened at the sight of their own blood, become even more courageous. Others, at the sight of any blood, let alone their own, fall down in a faint. The difference arises because people have different degrees of mental stability. Some are resolute, others quite cowardly. If you learn voluntarily to face minor problems, you will gradually become invincible to the different levels of suffering. It is the way of the wise that, faced with suffering, they never allow their minds to become disturbed.

When you wage war on the disturbing emotions, there is no doubt that you will have hardship and problems. In ordinary life no one goes to war expecting to experience peace and happiness. Some will be killed, many will suffer. When we wage war on the disturbing emotions, positive forces are quite weak, while the disturbing emotions are very powerful. There is no question that we will have to undergo hardship in this conflict. We must accept it without becoming discouraged. Voluntarily accept minor sufferings in order to gain victory over the real enemy like hatred that resides within. The person who wages such a war and gains victory is a real hero.

When we think of someone as an enemy, we normally tend to think of him or her as having independent existence. We also think of the harm done by that enemy as having independent existence. But if your enemy shoots and wounds you, it is actually the bullet that strikes your body, not the enemy. Just as a weapon is wielded by a person, so the person is controlled by the disturbing emotions residing within him or her. Normally we get angry with the person. Why do we never get angry with the basic cause of harm, the disturbing emotion? Why do we not get angry with the bullet that actually strikes us? Why do we hate only the person who stands between these two? You might answer that the person contributed to what happened. In that case, you should be angry with yourself, because you also contributed to what happened. If you had not been there, no one could shoot or otherwise harm you. The suffering you experience is not just a result of the weapon with which you were hurt; your own body is also responsible. The enemy provided the weapon, but you provided the target with your body. If someone hurts you, remember also that in the past you have similarly harmed other sentient beings and that as a result you are being harmed today. It is just the ripening of your own past misdeeds. Although you are being harmed by other sentient beings it is your own fault; you are responsible for it.

Whether someone is a friend or enemy, if you find them doing something inappropriate, you should remember that they do so as the result of many causes and conditions. Thus, there is no need for you to feel unhappy. If everything happened through the force of our own will without depending on anything else, then everyone would create happiness, because happiness is what everyone wants. But because of inattention and ignorance we engage in negative activities and inflict harm on ourselves. Under the influence of strong, disturbing emotions people will even kill themselves, despite their strong instinct for self-preservation.

Consequently, it is not surprising that sentient beings harm each other. When we see such things happen, instead of feeling anger we should generate compassion. Even if you cannot do that, what is the use of getting angry? If you say that people are harmful by nature, it is still not worth getting angry with them. It is the nature of fire to burn. If you get burned, there is no point in being angry with the fire. The best thing is to avoid getting burned. Since sentient beings are basically good by nature, and their bouts of anger and hatred are temporary, there is no point in getting angry with them. If the sky is suddenly filled with smoke, there is no reason to get angry at the sky. So why blame other people and get angry with them?

Your enemy harms you out of confusion and ignorance. If you too get angry out of confusion, both of you are at fault. How can you say one is correct and the other is not? The harm you experience today is provoked by your past misdeeds. If you do not like it, why did you commit those mistakes? Since everything is dependent on your actions, why get angry with someone else? As long as you do not purify your misdeeds, negative consequences are bound to occur.

By focusing on so-called enemies and meditating on love, compassion, and patience, we can purify many of our earlier misdeeds. Enemies give us the opportunity to accumulate virtuous qualities through our practice of patience, but by harming us they fall into unfavorable states of existence and remain there for a long time. Our own past negative deeds cause us to be harmed by the enemy. But as a result of harming us, the enemy accumulates negative deeds and suffers in the future. In this sense, it is actually we who are responsible for the accumulation of our enemy's negative deeds and we who send the enemy into unfavorable rebirths. This is how we indirectly destroy other sentient beings. The enemy provides us an opportunity to practice patience and thereby achieve Buddhahood, and in response we send him to hell. By providing us with the opportunity to cultivate patience, enemies actually benefit us. So, if we want to get angry with anyone, we should get angry with ourselves. And if we want to be pleased with anyone, it should be with our enemy.

The mind is not physical. No one can touch it, no one can harm it directly, and therefore no one can destroy it. If someone says something threatening, harsh, or unpleasant to you, it does you no actual harm, so there is no need to get angry. It is important that you just relax and stay calm and peaceful, paying no attention to what other people say. There is no need for you to feel unhappy or afraid. If you say that others' insults will hinder your prosperity, the response is that material goods have to be given up sooner or late anyway. If you can say that it is proper to get angry in order to obtain certain goods, the response is that however good something may be you will not keep it longer than this life. But the fruit of the anger that you have expressed to obtain it will stay with you for many lives.

Life can be compared to two dreams. In one dream you experience happiness for one hundred years and then wake up; in another dream you experience happiness for only a moment and then wake up. The point is that after you have awakened you cannot enjoy the happiness of your dreams again. Whether you live a long life or a short life, you will have to die. Whether or not you had many possessions and whether or not you enjoyed them for a long time, at the time of death you leave everything behind as if you had been robbed by a thief. You have to travel to the next world empty-handed.

The Communists in Tibet denigrate the Buddha, Dharma, and Sangha. They destroy stupas and temples out of disrespect. You should not be angry with such destruction, because even if someone damages images of the Buddha, the scriptures and stupas, they cannot do any harm to the actual Buddha, Dharma, and Sangha. If your friends and relatives are harmed by others, it is because of their past actions and many other causes and conditions. There is no place for anger. When embodied beings are harmed both by animate and inanimate phenomena, why should you be especially bent on retaliating against those who possess a mind?

When there is a lack of social harmony, remember that sentient beings have different dispositions, different ways of thinking, different ways of seeing things. This is natural. If some agitation, confusion, or disturbance arises, you should be able to see it as a result of your own action and so avoid resentment. Cultivate love and compassion instead. This is how to make yourself alert to accumulating virtuous deeds. For example, someone loses his or her house in a fire and moves elsewhere. Because of this experience, he or she will dispose of everything flammable. Likewise, when the fire of hatred arises in connection with something you are attached to, there is a danger of your merit being burned up. You should get rid of the object of attachment.

Sometimes we have to sacrifice minor pleasures for the sake of peace and happiness. For example, it would be better to pay a fine by way of punishment than to have your hand chopped off. If we are unable to tolerate even the minor sufferings of this life, why do we not refrain from anger, which gives rise to the torments of hell? For the sake of fulfilling our desires we risk suffering in hell for thousands of years. Such sufferings fulfill neither our own purpose nor the purposes of other sentient beings. On the other hand, if you appreciate the advantages of patience and the disadvantages of anger, undergoing hardship in order to overcome anger becomes tolerable. Putting up with such hardship is a source of great achievement. You will finally be able to remove the temporary and ultimate sufferings of sentient beings. Therefore, it is worth voluntarily accepting minor hardships and sufferings in order to accumulate immeasurable merit and achieve lasting peace and happiness.

If it makes someone happy to praise your own qualities, you welcome it. But you feel jealous to hear praise of the qualities of other people. This is inappropriate. If that is how you feel, what is the use of the prayer "May all sentient beings be happy"? It becomes just wishful thinking. If you really want all beings to be happy, and that is why you have cultivated the awakening mind, how can you be put out when they find some happiness through their own efforts? If you want sentient beings to be delivered to the exalted state of Buddhahood, why do you feel distressed when they obtain possessions and respect? If it is your responsibility to look after someone, but that person turns out to be able to look after himself, does it not make you happy? We say, "May all sentient beings have happiness and may they be separated from suffering." If sentient beings find happiness and reduce their suffering of their own accord, it is worth rejoicing about. But if you do not like sentient beings attaining peace and happiness, why talk about their attaining enlightenment?

People who are angry when others prosper have no awakening mind within them. Whether someone else is given something or not does not affect you. The gift does not belong to you and you will not obtain it, so why do you feel unhappy? Why do you abandon your merit, reputation, and good qualities by getting angry? Why do you give up the very qualities that allow you to achieve wealth and respect? Because of your own negative deeds, not only will you fail to strive for liberation, but you prefer to compete with those who have accumulated merit and receive gifts as a result. Is this appropriate?

Why do you feel happy when your enemy is miserable? Your simple wish for him to be unhappy cannot harm him. And even if he experiences suffering according to your wish, why should you feel happy? If it gives you satisfaction, such a negative attitude will only be a cause of your downfall. Once you are caught on the hook of the disturbing emotions, you will encounter great suffering. You will be impelled to live in hell. Neither praise nor reputation will turn into merit, nor will they prolong your life. They will give you neither strength nor good health. If you are able to decide what is useful and what is not, you will discover the benefit of respect and esteem. You may admit that there is no physical advantage but that you derive mental relief. If mental satisfaction is what you seek, why not take to your bed and get drunk? If all you want is temporary relief, you might as well take drugs.

Foolish people give up everything for the sake of fame. To be called heroes they let themselves be killed in battle. What is the use of sacrificing life and wealth for a mere name? People who worry about a decline in their name and fame are like those small children who work hard to construct a sand castle and cry the moment it collapses. Therefore, when someone praises you, do not feel too happy. Name has no essence; fame has no meaning. Attraction to name, fame, and respect will distract you from virtuous activities. For example, monks and nuns study the scriptures. Initially when they join a monastery they are humble. Gradually as they become more educated, they become scholars or earn the title of *geshe*. They acquire students and followers and completely change. Nowadays, I find that some teachers who have Western students get very puffed up. Business-people are similar. When they are successful in business they show it off by wearing expensive rings and watches. In Tibet, they would wear expensive earrings. In the long run, of course, earrings will only tear their ears and are of no other use.

When people who are supposed to be staying high in the mountains meditating gain a little reputation, they tend to leave their retreat and come down to the plains. Initially they may give advice to people about the need to meditate on impermanence and suffering. But gradually they themselves forget about these qualities and become inflated with negative qualities like jealousy and competitiveness. Weak and humble people, generally speaking, do not deceive and bully others. It is only in those people who have something to show off that jealousy and competitiveness arise. This is why praising ourselves and garnering respect are very dangerous. They stimulate the arising of negative qualities. Therefore, it is better to view those people who always find fault with us as actually protecting us. They prevent us from falling into unfavorable states of existence.

While we labor under the burden of disturbing emotions and negative actions, why do we need the additional burden of respect and reputation? Rather than getting angry with those people who would free us from the bondage of respect and reputation, we should value them. We are always bent on entering the path leading to suffering; then, as if we were blessed by the Buddha, our enemy comes and closes the door to hell by damaging the reputation we are so attached to. No fruit can arise without cause, and if the cause exists the fruit will follow. Here the fruitlike result is the practice of patience, while the cause is being harmed by other people. Therefore, patience arises because of the harm inflicted by your enemy. How can you say that such harm represents an obstruction of merit? Patience is possible only because of your enemy. For example, the presence of a beggar provides an opportunity for us to give. How could we call a beggar an obstruction to the practice of generosity?

There are many beggars in the world, so it is easy to practice generosity. But enemies and people who do us harm are generally rare, because if we do not harm other people, they will not normally harm us. This makes the circumstances for practicing patience quite rare. Our enemy provides us with the opportunity to practice patience without our having to harm anyone else, so we can rejoice in the opportunity and appreciate the value of our enemy. The enemy enhances our practice of the path of the bodhisattva because he contributes to the practice of patience.

Patience is extremely important for a bodhisattva, and patience can be developed only because of the presence of the enemy. Since our practice of patience is the result of both our own effort and the presence of the enemy, the resultant merit should first be dedicated to our enemy's happiness. You might say that even though the enemy provokes the practice of patience, it was not his or her intention to do so. He or she did not think, "I will give this person the chance to develop patience." But then why do we express respect for nirvana? Nirvana, the true cessation of suffering, has no intention or motive to benefit the person who achieves it. Why do we regard it as something precious? The enemy becomes your enemy because he or she has an intention to harm you. How could you practice patience if everyone, like a doctor, always tried to help you? It is your enemy who has enabled you to practice patience.

There are two objects in relation to whom we can collect merit. One is sentient beings, and the other is the Buddha. By pleasing the countless sentient beings, we can achieve the purposes of ourselves and others. We can achieve the perfection of positive qualities. Since sentient beings and the Buddhas have contributed equally to the attainment of Buddhahood, why do we show so much respect for the Buddha but ignore and bully sentient beings? The Buddhas, who are our ultimate objects of refuge, bring immeasurable benefit to countless sentient beings. The way to please them is to please sentient beings. There is no other way for us to repay their kindness. For the sake of helpless sentient beings, the Buddhas have given up even their bodies and have even entered into the unceasing suffering of hell. Likewise, bodhisattvas have generated the awakening mind and entered into spiritual practice only for the sake of sentient beings. We will be able to repay their kindness by helping sentient beings ourselves. Therefore, however much harm certain sentient beings may bring us, we should always react positively, trying to do only what will benefit. In order to carry out those activities that will please the Buddhas, we should regard ourselves as servants to other sentient beings. Even if sentient beings trample on our heads and kill us, we will not retaliate. The Buddhas and bodhisattvas possess great compassion, so there is no doubt that they will look after sentient beings. They have practiced for countless eons for the welfare of sentient beings. Since we are followers of the Buddha, why do we not become the protectors of sentient beings, why do we not pay them respect? This is the best practice to please the Buddhas and bodhisattvas and at the same time fulfill our own temporary and ultimate purposes. In this way all sentient beings, right down to the smallest insects, will become our friends. Wherever we live, the environment will be peaceful and calm. From life to life we will travel from one state of peace to another. Therefore, keeping a low profile, free from pride, and benefiting sentient beings is the best way of fulfilling our own purpose as well.

Normally, we take refuge in the Buddha, Dharma, and Sangha. With great purity of mind we pay our respects before images of the Buddhas and bodhisattvas. But when we see sentient beings, particularly those we think of as enemies, we generate jealousy and competitiveness. There is a great contradiction here. If we know someone we regard as a close friend, someone we love very much, we always try to avoid doing what would displease him or her. For example, you might like hot, spicy food but have a close friend who does not. If you really have regard for your friend when you invite him or her to dinner, you would prepare the food according to his or her taste. On the other hand, if you invite him or her to eat and prepare very hot, spicy food, full of chilies it is clear that you do not really regard that person as a genuine friend. So it seems that we do not really see the Buddha even as a close friend. His only thought and concern is for the welfare of sentient beings. What do we do? On the one hand we pay respect to the Buddha, but at the same time we completely neglect sentient beings. It is for the sake of sentient beings that the Buddha accumulated merit. It is for the sake of sentient beings that the Buddha generated the awakening mind. It is for the sake of sentient beings that the Buddha became enlightened, while we completely neglect sentient beings. It is unfortunate that in doing so we do not pay the Buddhas even the regard we would show a close friend.

Anger is the force that destroys your virtuous qualities; therefore, you should challenge anger and try to eliminate it. Instead of feeling unhappy and hostile toward your enemy, view him or her as your most cherished spiritual teacher, who teaches you the practice of patience. Normally we regard retaliating against our enemy as something worthy. Even from a legal point of view, you have a right to defend yourself. However, if you are trying to cultivate the awakening mind from the depth of your heart, you try to cultivate a strong positive mental attitude wishing to benefit sentient beings. Consequently, if you are able to develop a strong sense of compassion and loving-kindness toward your enemy, you will be able to generate similar loving-kindness and compassion toward all sentient beings.

It is like removing a huge stone that has been blocking the flow of water in a canal. Once you remove the stone, the water immediately starts to flow. Similarly, once you are able to cultivate loving-kindness and compassion toward your enemy, you will easily be able to cultivate loving-kindness and compassion toward all sentient beings. Therefore, if you are able to see the enemy as the supreme basis of the practice of patience, and if you are able to generate a stronger kind of compassion in relation to your enemy, this indicates success in your practice. By pleasing sentient beings we will not only be able ultimately to attain Buddhahood; even in this life we will earn a good reputation and find peace and happiness. We will make more friends. We will have no enemies. Life will be relaxed. While we remain wandering in the cycle of existence, as a result of practicing patience over many lives, we will have an attractive physical form. We will have a long life free from sickness, and we will attain the peace of the ruler of the universe.

We have found this precious human life and have met with the teaching of the Buddha. We have understood the advantages of the practice of patience and the disadvantages of anger. Whether or not we have the capacity to practice it now, at least we have understood that what has been explained is reasonable. Therefore, let us always follow this path, which guarantees peace, both now and in the future.

CHAPTER 6

Creating Self-Confidence

An important technique for enhancing the awakening mind is effort. Even in ordinary life we have to persevere if we are to achieve anything. Similarly, we need to make effort in our quest for spiritual realization. When laziness takes over, our pursuit of the Dharma will not advance. However, it is also important to be skillful in the way we apply our effort. We have an expression in Tibetan that says that effort should be steady, like a stream of running water. Effort implies that we take an interest in whatever we are doing. In this context, it is a question of taking joy in practicing the Dharma. Perseverance does not mean making a great deal of effort at certain times and being completely lax at others. Working steadily and consistently is the key to success.

Among many obstacles, discouragement is the major stumbling block to spiritual advancement. It indicates a loss of self-esteem and a lack of confidence. In order to counter such destructive attitudes, we must generate confidence and determination. Thinking about the Buddha nature is a very positive and powerful way of doing this. All sentient beings possess the Buddha nature, the seed of enlightenment. As far as this quality is concerned, we are each on a par with everyone else. We should draw inspiration from this innate potential and keep despondency and defeatism under control.

It is also useful to think about the Buddhas of the past. They did not gain spiritual realization spontaneously. Initially, they too were like any other ordinary sentient being, miserable and tormented by sufferings and afflictions. It was only after a great deal of perseverance in the practice of the Dharma over many lifetimes that they ultimately reached the state of full enlightenment. We should draw inspiration from accounts of their lives and follow in their footsteps by embarking on a proper spiritual path. It is extremely important that we do not allow laziness or a defeatist attitude to overwhelm us. On the contrary, we should cultivate a strong sense of self-confidence and have faith in our abilities and our potential.

What, then, is the definition of effort? Effort here means to rejoice in doing virtuous activities. You might exert yourself in various neutral or even negative deeds, but that would not count as effort in the Buddhist sense. The practice of effort involves generating a great sense of joy in developing virtuous qualities. An obstacle to that is laziness, of which there are several kinds, such as the laziness of procrastination, the laziness of being attached to meaningless activities, and the laziness that comes from the lack of confidence in one's abilities. These obstacles should be overcome.

The purpose of the teaching of the Buddha is to transform the mind. It is just like the kind of construction we do outside, except that it takes place within. We have to determine what the necessary circumstances and materials are, accumulate them, and then begin building. Likewise, we should identify the obstructive factors and remove them one by one. The principal obstacle to developing virtuous qualities is laziness, which means not being able to get anything done. If you become attached to some meaningless activity and are unable to do spiritual practice, that is one kind of laziness. If you think you will do it tomorrow or the day after tomorrow and put it off, that is another kind of laziness. If you think, "How can a person like me achieve success in spiritual practice?" that is yet another kind of laziness.

In order to overcome laziness, we have to know the causes that bring it about. Unless you remove its causes, you will not be able to overcome laziness. These causes include being fond of whiling away your time, becoming attached to too much relaxation or too much sleep, and not being dismayed by the sufferings of the cycle of existence. These are the three principal factors giving rise to laziness. The more you recognize the faults and sufferings of the cycle of existence, the stronger will be your attempt to overcome them. On the other hand, if you do not see the sufferings of the cycle of existence and if you feel happy as you are, you will not attempt to free yourself from them. As the great Indian scholar and adept Aryadeva said, "How can someone who is not discouraged by the faults of the cycle of existence take interest in nirvana? Like leaving home, it is also hard to leave worldly existence."

The disturbing emotions are compared to a kind of net. Once you fall into this net and are caught, you will be unable to free yourself from the hold of the disturbing emotions and you will fall into the jaws of death. One of the ways to counter laziness is to think about impermanence and the nature of death. Death has no compassion. Gradually, one by one, death takes us all. We constantly hear that someone has died in such and such a place or that someone has died on this or that road. Normally, when we hear about someone else's death, we tend to think that it was their turn to die and our turn will never come. We are like those foolish sheep whose companions are being led into the slaughterhouse but who still do not understand that they too are about to die. With no fear of death, we will simply go on enjoying ourselves and looking forward to sleep. When death will strike is unknown. It may be that death will visit you when you have just begun some undertaking. It makes no difference to death whether someone has just started some project or has half completed it. Death can catch us unawares at any time. But since we are going to die soon, while we are still alive we must try to accumulate merit. Once death overtakes us, it will be too late to eliminate laziness. At that time nothing can be done. Therefore, do not procrastinate. Do not put spiritual practice off until tomorrow or the next day; start immediately.

If you always procrastinate, putting off what you have to do until tomorrow or next year, even making a list of things you are going to do and, these days, storing it in your computer, one day you may suddenly be struck by a fatal illness. You will have to visit the hospital and take those awful medicines that you do not want to take. The surgeons may operate on you. Sometimes these white-clothed figures may be kind and compassionate; sometimes they operate on you as if they were simply opening up a machine that has no feelings.

Normally, when people are healthy and free from illness, they can boast that they do not believe in past or future lives. But as death looms, you recollect all your misdeeds. Your mind will be filled with remorse, pain, and unhappiness. You might even hear the sounds of hell nearby and wet your bed with fear. An acquaintance told me that when he was suffering a very severe sickness and in great pain, he heard many strange sounds and voices. Sometimes people faint with pain. Then, before coming around, it seems many people have an experience like traveling through a tunnel. That is when they have what are called near-death experiences. People who have accumulated severe negative deeds encounter many frightening experiences as a result of dissolution of the various physical elements of their bodies. When those who have accumulated a great deal of virtue are faced with the process of dying, they experience a sense of satisfaction and happiness.

Now, while we are still alive, we might be driven from our country by our enemies, but we still expect to be reunited with our relatives at some time. But at the time of death, you have to part from your friends and relatives forever. Even this precious body that has accompanied you everywhere will be taken from you. And once it is dead, people see your body as something dangerous, fearful, and horrible. That is why some great yogins have said that the frightful dead body is with us always, even while we are alive. You should see your human life as a vessel to cross the great ocean of suffering. Such a vessel will be very difficult to find in the future, so having found such a precious opportunity, in your bewilderment you should not just sleep.

The sublime teaching of the Buddha is a cause of infinite joy and happiness, but what could be more unfortunate than giving up this supreme path and getting distracted by causes leading to suffering? Take control of yourself, put procrastination behind you, and try to accumulate merit and wisdom to make your body and mind suitable for spiritual practice. This is comparable to preparing for war. First you must generate the self-confidence to fight. You must be determined to undergo all hardships and gain victory over all obstructive forces. Just as a military needs a strong force of well-armed, well-equipped, brave men, you should accumulate merit and wisdom. When you fight you should put your weapons to full use, aimed directly at the enemy. Likewise, whatever spiritual path you practice, you must wield the weapon of wisdom with mindfulness and attention. Consequently, you will defeat the enemy, laziness, and gain control over your body and mind, making it easier to engage in virtuous practice. To think that you have no capacity, intelligence, or potential is a great fault. Even in ordinary life you must have self-confidence to do whatever it is you want to do. People in the west are subject to what is called low self-esteem. I do not know whether it is present in Tibetan society or other cultures, but low self-esteem is very debilitating. Whether you are concerned with spiritual practice or the work of ordinary life, you must maintain confidence.

The Kadampa masters of the past had nothing to enjoy in their dry caves. They were so determined in their spiritual practice that they stayed there confidently and happily. They employed their entire being— their body, speech, and mind—in the practice of the Dharma. They never feared that because of their Dharma practice they would run out of food or other facilities and die. The Kadampa masters would think that even if they had to become beggars, they would rather pray for death than let themselves waste their time not practicing the Dharma. There is a danger of worrying that if you die, who will help you? Who will pray for you? But the Kadampa masters used to think, "Why should I bother whether someone helps me or not? I should prefer to die a natural death in a bare and empty cave just as animals and birds do." This is the kind of determination with which they would engage in their practice. They would say, "If I'm treated like an outcast, I will voluntarily accept it. If I have to join the company of dogs, I will do that. Like a dog I will wander here and there in pursuit of Dharma." Because of their determination they would finally attain Buddhahood.

If you are really going to practice the Dharma, you need strong determination and self-confidence. If you have no self-confidence, you will not achieve anything. Without expectation or doubt, enter into spiritual practice. Read the life of Milarepa. He gave up everything: his friends, his relatives, his possessions. In one of his famous songs he says, "If I fall sick unknown to my relatives and if I die unknown to my enemies, I, the yogin, will have fulfilled my wish." Even when we are concerned with fulfilling our responsibilities to one person or a few individuals, we have to have determination. Naturally, when we are cultivating the awakening mind, whose aim is the happiness of all sentient beings, we need especially strong determination.

If you say you want to cultivate the awakening mind for the sake of all sentient beings, but at the same time you say you do not feel capable, there is a contradiction. Generating mental courage does not mean you have to be proud. Pride and self-confidence are two different things. When you cultivate positive qualities like love, compassion, and the awakening mind, you should do so with self-confidence. The awakening mind is driven by the force of compassion, by concern for the welfare of all sentient beings. You are no longer bound by an ignorant misconception of self. You can wholeheartedly fight the disturbing emotions with confidence and determination.

With regard to the cause of Tibet, we must always think that we can succeed. We should have self-confidence. Let me tell you a story. Around 1979, during one of the more lenient periods when Tibetans were able to come and visit their relatives in exile, one man came to talk to me. He had been born in Lhasa and had lived there in the 1950s and witnessed the uprising. He told me that the Chinese are extremely clever and that their population is huge. They have so many weapons that there is nothing we can do. He was completely discouraged. I think the sound of weapons being fired in the 1950s was still in his ears. Then there was an old monk from the Dokham area. He had seen the military operations being carried out in those areas. Whole villages were wiped out, and many people were massacred. I told him that when we are so few and they are so many, these things will definitely take place. Then I asked him what would happen if one Tibetan were to fight one Chinese. He laughed and said that then it would be easy, that we could play with them in the palms of our hands. That was his kind of mental courage. It is not a matter of pride, but it is important to have self-confidence, to think that you can do it. When problems arose in 1959, we Tibetans were in a very difficult position. The entire Tibetan population is only 6 million, so things were quite discouraging. But since 1959 we have never given up, because we are fighting for a true cause, a just cause. We have never lost our determination to achieve our aim. Even though more than forty years have passed since the Communist Chinese first came to Tibet, instead of disappearing, the Tibetan cause is gaining momentum. We are getting more support, and there is a possibility of achieving something before long.

How can we maintain self-confidence and not let ourselves get discouraged? The compassionate Buddha, who tells only the truth and nothing else, has put it this way. Even those sentient beings living an inferior kind of life, like bees, flies, and other insects, whose physical existence is weak, have the Buddha nature. If they make the effort, even such weak sentient beings can evolve over many lifetimes and ultimately achieve the unsurpassable state of Buddhahood, so difficult to attain. This is what the Buddha taught. All sentient beings possessing a luminous mind have the potential to attain Buddhahood. However weak they may be, and no matter how overwhelming the suffering they encounter, they all have the potential to attain Buddhahood. If this is so, when we have been born as human beings and know to some extent what is beneficial and what is harmful, if we do not give up the practices of a bodhisattva, why should we not attain Buddhahood?

The great spiritual masters of the past in India and Tibet were also human beings like us. They were able to achieve such high spiritual attainments because they possessed the Buddha nature and because they had found a human life. We also have the Buddha nature, and we also have found a precious human life, so there is nothing that we cannot achieve. For example, read the biography of Tsong-kha-pa. Read how he worked in order to gain the different stages of spiritual development. In some of his compositions from the early part of his life, Tsong-kha-pa himself writes about not having fully understood the viewpoint of the Middle Way. This clearly indicates that he was not omniscient or fully realized then. But he engaged in the twin practices of accumulating merit and developing wisdom. As a result, the compositions from the later part of his life are profound, deep, decisive, and conclusive. It is very helpful to read stories such as these. They give us hope in the possibility of attaining higher realization.

Let me tell you the story of one of the Buddha's past lives. You should understand that Buddhists do not believe in a creator. This means that Buddhahood is not given by some higher being but is attained by following a proper path. Shakyamuni, the historical Buddha, did not reach enlightenment in just one lifetime. He engaged in virtuous and extensive deeds in many previous lives. The tales of his previous births tell of his great practices while ascending the spiritual path. In this particular story, he was born as a prince. His name was Vishvantara, "Liberator of the Universe," and his father was king Samgaya.

Vishvantara was not merely an ordinary being but a reincarnation of a bodhisattva whose sole aim was to alleviate the sufferings of sentient beings. Since poverty was one of the major causes of misery, he engaged primarily in the practice of giving. In addition to being kind, his father, King Samgaya, was a man of courage and wisdom. He was well versed in the philosophy of the Vedas. Vishvantara in many ways took after his father. Fear was unknown to him. He was kind to everyone and placed great stock in compassion. He had the manners of a prince, yet he was equally accessible to the people of the palace and to the common citizens.

From an early age he took a close interest in spiritual matters. He had great faith in and devotion to the Buddhas and bodhisattvas, and he made regular offerings to them. He sought out spiritual masters and listened to their teachings. In true Buddhist tradition, he first listened to spiritual teachings and subjected them to logical scrutiny. Then, by way of contemplation and meditation, he put them into practice. Spiritual teachings were not just dry philosophy for him. He understood them as instructions to guide his day-to-day life. Because of the virtuous imprints in his stream of consciousness, he made speedy progress. He cultivated a disciplined mind and thoroughly controlled his disturbing emotions. This naturally made him calm, peaceful, and full of joy.

He immersed himself in study of the five major sciences: grammar, medicine, the arts, logic, and the inner science, or Buddhist philosophy. At the same time, he trained in the ways of managing the kingdom, from both the administrative and diplomatic points of view. In due course he became a scholar of some substance and began to teach other bright young students. Affection was showered upon him from all sides. He made great efforts to meet the needs of his people. He was preoccupied by his attempts to eradicate poverty, but he still took interest in the affairs of the merchants. There was a great sense of peace and harmony among his people.

Vishvantara possessed great wealth, and, being a prince, he enjoyed power, authority, and prestige. Yet, because of his spiritual inclinations and faith in the Dharma, he never indulged in worldly concerns, nor did he abuse his power and position. It is common knowledge that wealth and authority in the hands of the ignorant will harm both self and others. We can observe from day to day how many narrow-minded people spoil themselves with too much money. They are arrogant and shortsighted, and they show no respect for other people's concerns. Yet the prince was not like this. He had control of his senses and was disciplined in his behavior. He had the dignity of a prince, yet he was kind, sympathetic, and sincere in serving the interests of his people.

When your motivation is pure and the cause is good, wealth and power have a role to play. They can certainly help you achieve your goals. The important factor is your attitude. Vishvantara was a highly evolved person, and by seeing the disadvantages of life in the cycle of existence he had developed a true determination to be free of it. At the same time he had an equal sense of loving-kindness and compassion toward all sentient beings. His practice of the six perfections, generosity in particular, was motivated by powerful compassion. A bodhisattva's compassion is unconditional, and yet he or she feels even more concerned for those in pain and misery. The prince was a highly intelligent and sympathetic person, but we should not forget that we too have the potential and required conditions to transform ourselves into good human beings. We should not let the opportunity slip away.

The prince was in reality a bodhisattva with high ideals. Although he was involved in both spiritual and temporal activities, everything he did was intended to benefit as many sentient beings as possible, directly and indirectly. His motivation was not polluted by selfish concerns. Because of his kindness and compassion, Vishvantara was accustomed to giving to the poor and the needy. He had both great wealth and the power and authority to dispose of it as he wished. He was not bound by the fetters of miserliness. He was properly aware of what to give and when to give it. This is important; without this awareness, even if you mean well, you can make mistakes in your giving. This is also why kindness needs to be balanced by wisdom.

Mere giving does not constitute practice of the perfection of generosity. There are certain criteria that must be fulfilled. You should never disparage the person who is asking for your help and generosity. On the contrary, you should be pleased to come across someone asking for alms. You should see him or her as a teacher who is giving you the chance to develop your generosity. You should give according to the recipient's needs, in terms of both the gift and the timing. There are certain things, such as alcohol, poison, and weapons, that we are prohibited from giving. The practice of giving requires that you be astute in giving appropriately to each particular person.

Vishvantara had a pure and wholesome motivation; he gave universally and unconditionally. He made no discrimination between one person and the next but gave to each according to their needs. This attracted many people from outside the kingdom to come and beg for alms. The prince was deeply moved by people's pain and poverty, which only served to intensify his generosity. He established many places where alms were handed out regularly in an organized way and personally supervised their distribution. Those who came to beg were satisfied, and there were no complaints. Vishvantara took increasing delight in being able to give, and as his determination became firmer his motivation became purer.

You can develop the inspiration to engage in virtuous practices like giving by reflecting on their benefits. When you give, you are able to fulfill the needs of the poor and needy and relieve them of the suffering of poverty. Seeing their satisfaction automatically generates joy in your heart. This joy in turn creates an atmosphere of peace around you and increases your own and other's well-being. A generous person gains respect and recognition in society, and his or her reputation spreads far and wide. In the longer run, the consequence of giving is that you will be rich in your future lives. Generosity gives rise to a creative mind.

Vishvantara was convinced of the benefits of the practice of generosity and was highly motivated to develop it. He felt that he could give away his limbs or even his entire body if the need arose. This feeling arose from a deep sense of kindness and compassion for all miserable sentient beings. His motivation was so strong that it caused an earthquake whose impact was felt even in the palace of Indra, the king of gods. When Indra looked into the cause of the tremor, he discovered that it was due to the power of Vishvantara's generous motivation.

Wanting to test the purity of the prince's motivation, Indra set out to meet him in the guise of an old, blind brahmin. When the opportunity arose he approached Vishvantara, saying, "I am an old blind man who has come from far away after facing many hazards on the road. You are a generous prince with two eyes. With one eye you can see everything. I beg you to give me your second eye." This peculiar request gave Vishvantara pause. He carefully weighed the benefits against the disadvantages. Above all, he was concerned about whether such a gift could really be of help. But the old man was adamant and repeated that no hardship was greater than blindness. The prince decided that he ought to help the old man, which would also give him the opportunity to fulfill his commitment to the practice of giving. He told the man he would give him his eye.

When the courtiers in the palace heard of his decision, they were very worried. They could see no point in what he was going to do and pleaded with him to change his mind. They suggested that instead he could give the old man any amount of money from the royal treasury. Vishvantara was more concerned about keeping his word, and the courtiers failed to persuade him to change his decision. Generating a determined and kindly motivation, he gave the old man both his eyes. As soon as it was done, Indra manifested himself and applauded the prince's selfless action. He then proclaimed that if Vishvantara had truly made the gift out of a pure and selfless motivation, his eyes should be restored. Immediately Vishvantara found he could see more clearly than ever. Indra disappeared, leaving the prince filled with joy and satisfaction. His faith in the teachings had become even more stable and profound.

The courtiers could not believe what had occurred but were overjoyed to know that no permanent damage had been done to the prince's sight. Vishvantara continued to be generous, and his reputation extended far and wide. Under very difficult circumstances he gave away a prized elephant. It was one of the kingdom's most precious possessions, symbolizing its sovereignty and power. The news spread quickly through the palace and beyond. Both ministers and common citizens were offended by what the prince had done. They took their complaints to the king and argued forcefully that the prince was much too absorbed in spiritual pursuits and was unfit to succeed to the throne. This put the king in a dilemma. He loved his son and had cherished great hopes for him. But after careful thought and reflection, he decided that the interests of the kingdom and palace took precedence and that he would have to banish the prince.

Accordingly, the ministers conveyed the royal verdict to the prince. Vishvantara did not take it badly—in fact, he seems to have been the least upset of anyone. He replied that he was willing to abide by his father's decision, but he wanted to depart alone, leaving behind his wife and two children. However, the princess Madri insisted on accompanying him. Therefore, Vishvantara, his wife, and his children set out from the palace, taking only what they were given by his father. As they were leaving, the prince told the ministers that the community of monks and nuns should be respected and their needs fulfilled. He added that the palace should continue to look after the poor and destitute. Finally, he assured them that the kingdom and its people would always be in his prayers.

The prince thought that a secluded place in the forest would be the proper place for him to pursue his spiritual goals. As he and his family traveled, they met people who asked them for alms. The prince was still as generous as he had been in the palace and gave away their belongings one by one. When they came to the end of their journey, Vishvantara had given away almost everything they owned, including the chariot and horses. The prince and the princess reached the clearing in the forest, each carrying a child in their arms. The children were still small, which made life for the princess all the more difficult. Vishvantara saw his new life from a different angle. He thought it would give him an opportunity to meditate and gain spiritual insight, which had not been possible while he lived in the palace.

Such a life was hard for a family. As they had no resources, the children were constantly hungry, and their mother suffered immensely. Since the prince was absorbed in meditation, she had to go out to gather food. Even under these circumstances, Vishvantara's reputation for generosity continued to grow. It soon reached the ears of an old couple who had no children. They thought that if they were to ask the prince to give them his children, they could employ them as servants. They chose a time when the princess was away in search of food and approached the prince to make their request. Vishvantara was put on the spot. He dearly loved his children, but he was also fully committed to his practice of generosity. The situation became very difficult as the old people pressed their demand.

Vishvantara did not want to disappoint anyone who requested anything of him, yet he was very concerned about his children's future. He tried to come to a compromise. He told them that if they were to take his children to the king, he would ransom them in exchange for money. That would leave them well off for the rest of their lives. The old couple responded to this that the king might instead imprison them. Acknowledging this possibility, the prince was literally dumb-founded. Gathering up his courage, Vishvantara asked the old couple to wait until the children's mother returned so she could bid them farewell. Even this condition was not acceptable to them. They pointed out that the mother might well interfere and obstruct the prince's practice of generosity and prevent the old couple from obtaining two useful servants. Reluctantly, Vishvantara acceded and gave away his delightful children to fulfill the old couple's wishes. When the princess returned and discovered the loss of her children, she fell down in a faint. Vishvantara too sank into depression.

When they recovered, they consoled each other, and Vishvantara renewed his determination to work for the benefit of all sentient beings. While they continued to live as before, secluded in the forest, Indra came to hear of Vishvantara's gift of his children. The king of the gods was astounded. He decided to test the greatness of Vishvantara's heart once again and approached him disguised as a prince. Vishvantara received the stranger very cordially and asked how he could help him. The stranger told him he had heard a great deal about his reputation for generosity, adding, "If I heard correctly, you have even given away your own children." The stranger continued to praise the prince, telling him that his commitment to openhearted generosity was renowned in every corner of the world. It was said that he had never disappointed anyone. Finally, he came to his own special request. Vishvantara told him to spell out his needs, and that he would try to fulfill them. The stranger replied, "I am a lonely man with no one to live for. Kindly give me your wife to comfort me and give meaning to my existence."

Vishvantara was very confused. He was at a loss to know why his goodness of heart should be put to such a test. His loving wife was his sole source of hope and support. His very survival was at stake. She loved him, and parting would mean unbearable pain. Vishvantara was speechless. Even under such stress he remembered that he had set himself the spiritual goal of liberating all sentient beings from misery. Madri, his wife, pleaded with him not to make her leave him. Vishvantara too knew well how hard such a break would be. But the man pressed his demand, arguing that if Vishvantara failed to give him his wife, it would amount to a breach of his commitment. He said that he himself would lose his will to live. Vishvantara tried to console his wife. He explained the long-term advantages of generosity in the interest of sentient beings. He also asserted that they should not disappoint a suffering person face to face. Finally, Vishvantara agreed to give his dear wife to the lonely, helpless man.

Vishvantara's courage and goodness of heart were not in vain. Great good fortune and joy were in store for him, his loving wife, and their children. The man took Madri's hand, but as they walked away he vanished and Indra himself appeared in his place. The king of the gods praised Vishvantara's virtuous deed, calling him a lion among men. He predicted that the prince's greatness of heart would gain universal recognition and admitted that he had come only to test his commitment to generosity. Repeating his admiration for Vishvantara and his wife,

Indra told them it was time for them to return to the royal place. He also arranged for the old couple to meet them there with their two children. Finding the prince, the princess, and his grandchildren on his doorstep, the king was overjoyed. There was merrymaking throughout the kingdom. Not long after, Vishvantara succeeded to his father's throne. He assumed the role of Dharmaraja, religious king, and created great peace and harmony among his people.

Stories like these are not just tales to please the ears. We must learn and draw inspiration from them. There is a Tibetan saying: "The biographies of the exalted masters of the past should be seen as spiritual instructions for their followers." The principal theme of the bodhisattva Vishvantara's life is the practice of generosity. Generosity is particularly recommended for beginners on the spiritual path. Giving is a virtue that benefits both the giver and receiver. The giver is able to create merit, which will produce happiness and fortune in the future. The receiver gains relief from the pangs of want and poverty. The practice of giving has two aspects: making offerings to the Buddhas and fulfilling the material needs of the poor. It is essential that we begin by developing a will to give backed by kind and positive thoughts. We should give whatever we can afford, but it is equally important that, like Vishvantara, we mentally commit ourselves to the practice of generosity over and over again. This is how we strengthen our willpower and determination to give.

Over countless eons, as a human being or as an animal, you have involuntarily encountered many such sufferings and hardships. There is no suffering that you have not encountered due to the force of the disturbing emotions. Your body might have been butchered or bought, burned or flayed. Even though you have faced them before, such problems are a kind of self-torture, because they are the results of your disturbing emotions. But far from helping you attain Buddhahood, these hardships did not even contribute to your wealth or long life. Despite the fact that you have faced countless sufferings over beginningless time, these hardships did not put an end to suffering, so they really are a kind of torture.

However, if you set your sights on Buddhahood, direct your mind toward it, and make some effort, whether you face hardship or not, you will have a definite goal. Hardship is limited in pursuit of Buddhahood, because such hardship yields spiritual progress. And the more you practice, the more realizations you will gain. Then, because of your mental attitude, because you will achieve some spiritual quality, even the so-called hardships can be easily dealt with. Therefore, as you reach the higher levels of spiritual development, a time will come when you may sacrifice your whole body without regarding it as a hardship. Through the power of your practice and the power of strengthening your mental attitude you can put an end to suffering.

There is no end to the sufferings you encounter in the cycle of existence. Imagine you have been shot in the stomach and you are in great pain. In order to remove the bullet and counter the pain, you have to undergo surgery. Although it may create certain other problems, you gladly accept the pain of surgery in order to overcome the problem of having a bullet in your stomach. Nowadays, operations are performed to completely remove some parts of the body and transplant others. Sometimes you have to give up parts of your body to save your own life. In order to avoid a greater pain, we are prepared to accept lesser degrees of pain. Although physicians, medication, and surgery all make us feel uncomfortable, we are prepared to put up with them to overcome illness. Clearly, in order to overcome countless sufferings we should be patient with minor hardships.

Buddha Shakyamuni is like a supreme physician, whose aim is to make all sentient beings attain Buddhahood. He has taught a very smooth path, and if you follow that smooth technique you will be able to cure yourself of immeasurable pain. The Buddha is like an excellent guide. If we have to cross a high and difficult mountain, we cannot make a path or construct a road straight uphill. We cannot force a vehicle to climb straight uphill. In order to reach the top we have to follow a zigzag path that will gradually bring us there. Similarly, the Buddha taught different levels of path according to the capacity of his followers. These paths can gradually lead all sentient beings to the attainment of Buddhahood.

The practice of generosity is an example. The Buddha taught us first to make gifts of food and so forth. Once we become familiar with such practices of giving, a time will gradually come, as your compassion and your wisdom grow stronger, when you can easily offer your own body or flesh. A time will come when you will be able to regard your own body no differently from food. Once you are able to see your body in that way, what kind of hardship will it be to give it up? However, unless and until your mind is trained, it will be extremely difficult.

Sometimes when watching television I have seen seemingly cruel scientific experiments being done on animals. You can see how scientists open up the brains of animals while they are still alive. I cannot watch; I have to close my eyes immediately. This is a clear sign that I am not used to such things, whereas those who are used to them do not hesitate. Similarly, when I see chickens kept in cages just outside restaurants I feel sad, but for the people who kill and cook them, the chickens are no more than vegetables. Right now the willingness to go to hell for the sake of one sentient being may seem horrifying, but as you gradually get used to the idea it will become easy.

Bodhisattvas who have eliminated their negative deeds feel no physical suffering. And because of their practice of method and wisdom, particularly wisdom, they feel no mental unhappiness. Because of the misconception of self we do misdeeds, which bring harm to our body and mind. Because of merit we will experience physical well-being, and because of wisdom we will have joy. Therefore, even if they have to stay in the cycle of existence, the compassionate ones are never discouraged. Because of their mental courage, the courage of the awakening mind, bodhisattvas are able to eliminate negative deeds accumulated in the past and collect oceanlike merit. Therefore, they are regarded as superior to those intent on personal liberation. For this reason, without discouragement you should mount the horse of the awakening mind and travel from peace to peace. If you really posses such a mind, how could you become discouraged?

In order to fulfill the wishes of sentient beings, you should accumulate the powers of aspiration, stability, joy, and knowing when to stop. Aspiration is the wish to practice, and having mental stability means not giving up the practice. Joy is to take delight in the practice. Knowing when to stop means that when you are tired, you should rest.

The time to stop is when you are being successful, not when you have achieved nothing. If you force yourself to practice when your mind is unwilling, you will come to dislike even the sight of the place where you do your meditation. Therefore, in the beginning you must be skillful in your approach. When you start to meditate, at the beginning of each session, you should always be fresh and try to enjoy it. Therefore, resting should serve to strengthen your subsequent practice. You should not force yourself to the point of total exhaustion. Take a break before you get completely exhausted.

Our own and other sentient beings' faults are immeasurable. They must be destroyed. Fault here refers to the disturbing emotions and the obstructions to liberation and enlightenment. To remove just one of these innumerable faults might take countless eons. But we have not begun to eliminate even a part of that fault. Yet abiding in this cycle of existence, full of suffering, is heartbreaking. We and other sentient beings must achieve countless qualities in order to become Buddhas, but cultivating just one quality might take countless eons. Yet we have not begun to familiarize ourselves with even a fraction of those qualities. It is strange how we waste our lives. We have not made offerings to the Buddhas. We have not contributed to the flourishing of the Buddha's teachings. We have not fulfilled the wishes of the poor and have not granted the gift of fearlessness to the fearful. Neither have we given the bread of peace and happiness to the helpless. When we were in the womb we gave our mothers pain. Right from the beginning we have been a source only of suffering. We have achieved no purpose as human beings because we have had no aspiration toward spiritual practice. If you are intelligent, how could you avoid such an aspiration?

You must cultivate self-confidence and meditate. Before you embark on spiritual practice you must examine it and decide whether you should start it or not. If you think you will be unable to do it, it would be better not to start. Having started you should not give up. Otherwise, not being able to complete your spiritual practice will become a habit. Not only in this life, but in future lives too, because of your habit of giving up your spiritual practice, unwholesome deeds and sufferings will multiply. You will find yourself unable to complete your other activities, and it will take a long time to achieve any result. Therefore, you must first examine whether you can achieve what you are setting out to do. Having determined to start a virtuous practice, you should complete it.

Because of disturbing emotions, ordinary beings are powerless even to fulfill their own purposes. They are involuntarily undergoing a kind of self-torture. In order to earn a small amount of money, some people have to spend days and nights working; others have to be aggressive and deceitful. They are involved with inferior kinds of activity, but nevertheless they enter into it gladly. We have made a commitment to fulfill the purposes of all sentient beings, so how can we sit back? We need to have a positive sense of self-confidence, but we should not act out of pride or courage with a negative motivation. Pride in the negative sense of self-importance is a disturbing emotion that must be removed. If we let ourselves become discouraged and lose our self-confidence, disturbing emotions can easily intrude upon us.

We must keep up our self-confidence, thinking that we are children or followers of the lionlike Buddha. This kind of positive self-confidence counters our negative sense of pride. There is nothing negative about feeling confident that we can do whatever needs to be done. If our minds are filled with self-confidence and we see the disturbing emotions as our enemy, we will be prepared to undergo hardship to overcome our pride. That kind of self-confidence is nothing to be ashamed of. Those who gain victory over pride but retain a sense of self-confidence are called the brave and victorious ones. They will be able to attain Buddhahood and fulfill the wishes of sentient beings. If we have that kind of self-confidence, even when we feel surrounded by a host of disturbing emotions, they will not harm us, just as a group of foxes cannot harm a lion. Just as human beings guard their eyes despite being confronted by other problems, even if it leads to further hardship, never let yourself be overpowered by disturbing emotions. It would be better to be burned, killed, or beheaded than to bow down to the enemy of disturbing emotions.

You must cultivate the power of joy. People who follow the ways of a bodhisattva engage happily and joyfully in their practice, just as a child happily enters into play. You must enter into the way of life of a bodhisattva without becoming complacent. Ordinary beings engage in many activities to produce a little contaminated happiness, because they are not sure whether they will achieve the expected results or not. There may be only a fifty-fifty chance of their achieving what they want, but still, ordinary people work very hard. However, if you follow the bodhisattva's way of life, it is 100 percent certain that you will find lasting peace and happiness. The bodhisattva's way of life is pleasing and useful to you and all other sentient beings.

No lasting satisfaction can be derived from sensual pleasures or desirable objects. These things are like honey smeared on the sharp blade of a sword. When you lick it, you may be able to taste the honey's sweetness, but at the same time you lose your tongue. But when you work toward the lasting peace of liberation, you will achieve great merit and peace. Without being complacent, work to accumulate the merit that results in the peace of liberation. If you do so, you will be able to bring your efforts to a conclusion. Therefore, enter happily into the bodhisattva's way of life, just as an elephant scorched by the sun plunges joyfully into the coolness of a lake.

CHAPTER 7

The Meditator's Practice

One of the best ways of controlling the mind is by concentration. On the basis of single-pointed concentration we can remove the grosser levels of the disturbing emotions. Concentration is not very important by itself, but it plays an essential role on the path. Whatever meditation you do, whether it concerns mundane or transcendental qualities, your achievement is dependent on single-pointed concentration. When you achieve single-pointed concentration, you can focus your mind on any object. By combining special insight into emptiness with the practice of the calmly abiding mind, you will be able to destroy the disturbing emotions. To cultivate such a special insight, you must first cultivate concentration.

In order to achieve single-minded concentration, you should first assemble the necessary causes and conditions. Physically, you should stay in an isolated place. It is not good to meet too many people and indulge in an unending stream of gossip. Stay in a place where you do not have to associate with many people. The thorn disturbing concentration is sound. Therefore, you should stay in a place that is quiet, free from noise and commotion. The most important thing is to free your mind of disturbances. If your mind is free from conceptual thoughts and your body is free from agitation, you will face no distractions, but the person whose mind is distracted is like someone living between the jaws of the disturbing emotions. In order to stop discursive thoughts from arising, you must reflect on the faults of attachment and desire.

Why should one impermanent entity generate attachment for another? For example, if two people were about to be executed, would they become attached to each other? Similarly, if two people are suffering from a fatal illness, it is absurd that these two people should get attached to each other or fight one another. Therefore, for one impermanent person to get attached to another makes no sense. Friends and relatives are not permanent. They change from moment to moment. And because you are attached to them, you destroy the possibility of finding the unchanging state of liberation. Because of the mind's unstable nature, sentient beings can become your friends one moment and a moment later become your enemies. Because of your own attachment, you also contribute to the development of attachment in others.

If you have great attachment but meet with nothing pleasant, you will have no mental pleasure and no mental stability. Even if you meet with pleasant things, they will give you no satisfaction. You will generate further craving and attachment, which in turn will bring you harm. Therefore, as long as you have attachment within you, whether you meet with pleasant objects or not, you will have no happiness. Therefore, at the outset you must put a stop to attachment within.

There is a saying that if you lie on a mountain of gold, then gold will rub off on you. If you lie on a mountain of mud, you will get muddy. And if you associate with childish beings, you too will engage in childish, unwholesome activities. By praising yourself, defaming others, and involving yourself in talk pleasing to the beings in the cycle of existence, you will be dragged into unfavorable states of existence. You will be unable to renounce the cycle of existence. As bees extract honey from flowers without being attached to the flowers or their colors, you should just take what is necessary for your spiritual practice and remain detached from worldly concerns.

Beings whose minds are confused and who are attached to material goods and to praise will have to encounter suffering a thousand times worse than the displeasure of attachment. Therefore, the wise do not let themselves get attached, because from attachment arises fear. And sooner or later you have to give up whatever you are attached to. There is a saying that whatever has been gathered together will be dispersed and whatever is high will one day fall. Even if you acquire wealth and excellent possessions, even if many pleasant things are said about you and you become famous, you cannot take them with you when you die. When there are people who criticize and defame you, why should you feel particularly pleased if someone praises you? And when there are people who praise you, why should you get so upset when someone criticizes? Sentient beings, because of their karmic condition and their mental interests and dispositions, are so fickle that even the Buddhas are not able to please them.

Because of his wonderful physical, mental, and verbal qualities, countless people were attracted to Buddha Shakyamuni, and yet there were still some people who said bad things about him. In that case, what does it matter if they speak badly about ordinary beings like us, who are completely under the sway of disturbing emotions? Therefore, give up trying to please worldly beings. When someone has no friends, people will laugh at him, saying it is because he is not well behaved. If he has many friends and visitors, people will again speak badly of him, saying, "Oh, he is such a flatterer." People always have something to say. Whatever you do, it is very difficult to live at ease with childish beings.

Unless they get what they want, immature beings will be unhappy. Even the Buddha has said that it is difficult to trust or befriend them. Since we face so many problems when we associate with worldly beings, the Buddha has recommended the qualities of remaining in an isolated place. There are many advantages to staying away from the hustle and bustle of cities and towns and remaining in an isolated place. In the forest or high up in the mountains there are only wild animals and beautiful plants and flowers. These animate and inanimate objects will not say bad things to you. Unlike human beings, they are not carried away either by suspicion or by high expectations. You need have no worries about coming to harm in such surroundings. Such companions are easy to associate with.

How pleasant it would be to stay somewhere like a cave, an empty temple, or under a tree. If you could stay in such a place without ever having to return to the same old life, if you could stay in an empty cave with no other human companions, then you would not have disturbing emotions like attachment. When the place where you stay has no owner and by nature is wide and open, it will bring you joy. How good it would be if you could enjoy such an opportunity.

In such a place you do not need many possessions. Those who are ordained need only a clay begging bowl and discarded rags to clothe themselves. When you stay in such a place, because you do not have many possessions, you do not have to hide them. People normally remain very alert when they are wealthy, worrying that other people will see their possessions. They worry that their belongings will become smelly and rotten during the monsoon rains, or that they will be chewed up by rats. They constantly have to conceal their goods and worry about preserving them.

When we Tibetans first came into exile, most of us had only one or two boxes of belongings and nothing else. It was very convenient. When I was in Lhasa we used to have many things that had belonged to the previous Dalai Lamas. A lot of work went into preserving them: putting their clothes out in the sun, and so forth. The disciplinarians of the different monasteries used to ask monks not to keep many belongings, so they would be able to remain like a single stick of incense. It is said that you should live in such a way that all you own is what you stand up in. That means you have nothing to carry and nothing to hide.

The Kadampa masters used to say that although ordained beings were able to free themselves from a householder's life, they tended to imprison themselves again in a second kind of home. This means that if, after getting ordained as a monk or a nun, you continue to gather belongings, you will once again get involved in how to protect them. Those who own nothing and just stay in an empty cave have nothing to hide. If you have nothing to hide, you have nothing to fear. There is a story about the people who heard that bandits were coming to raid their village. They all ran away with whatever wealth they could carry, and whatever else they could hide, they hid. But one man did nothing and just stood there watching the others. When they asked him why he was not running like them, he said, "I possess nothing, so I have nothing to hide."

In order to overcome attachment, contemplate the fact that at death we must part from our close friends and relatives, our possessions, and even our body. When you are born, you are born alone. Likewise, when you die, you die alone. No one else can share your suffering. Birth and death are the two most important occasions in our lives, during which no one can help us and no one can share our suffering. Travelers stay overnight in a guesthouse and then move on. Likewise, as we travel through the cycle of existence, as we have been doing from beginningless time, our momentary births are like the traveler's overnight stop. Our lives are like a momentary halt, for we are not going to live forever. Sooner or later you will die and your body will be carried away by four pallbearers while your friends and relatives lament and suffer around you. If at that time you regret having been unable to do positive things and having done many negative things, it will be far too late. Therefore, before things reach that point, retire to the forest and practice. In the stories of the great adepts of the past, those who attained high realizations always stayed in peaceful isolated places. There are not many accounts of people who attained great realization in a city or town.

What is the benefit of meditating in such an isolated place? You will not have so-called friends and relatives close by. When you have them around you, although you may want to practice and remain peaceful and quiet, your friends will not let you. When you live among ordinary people, there might be some people—your enemies, or people you do not like—the mere sight of whom makes you upset. If you stay in the forest or an isolated place, you will face no problems with either friends or enemies. If you live in solitude in an isolated place, already regarded as dead, then when you die there will be no one around you to lament. The birds and animals who are your companions will not lament, nor will they do you any harm. In such circumstances you will be able to do virtuous practices such as recollecting the qualities of the Buddha, meditating on emptiness, or doing tantric practice. There will be no one to distract you.

When attachment and anger manifest within us, if we are able to fulfill our wishes we will feel some kind of temporary relief and satisfaction, but if we were devoid of attachment and anger we would have enduring satisfaction and contentment. The fortunate abide in a peaceful forest free of disturbing emotions and arguments. The environment provides a calming experience similar to the soothing effect of sandalwood or the light of the moon. In such a peaceful forest you can meditate undisturbed in a pleasant house made of stone. There you can reflect on what will benefit other sentient beings. If you get tired of the place, without hesitation, you can move somewhere else in the forest.

It is very good to be able to stay in such a place. You will rely on no one; you will be completely free and independent and have no attachment. You will have no occasion to discriminate among beings, saying this is my enemy, my leader, or my friend. You will lead a contented life, happy with whatever you get. Even the king of the gods does not lead such a life. Thinking about the qualities of living in such an isolated place, you must dispel disturbing conceptual thoughts and meditate on the awakening mind.

Therefore, you should stay alone in such a solitary place, a place in the forest, where you will not have to undergo much hardship, where there is peace and happiness, where you will be free from distraction. You must abandon any thoughts of helping your friends and harming your enemies. You must think only of achieving Buddhahood for the sake of all sentient beings. You must focus single-mindedly on that as your motive in order to enter into meditative equipoise and transform your mind through the cultivation of wisdom.

In this world and beyond, desire brings distraction. Whether you desire some object or simply fame and good reputation, your desire can become a cause for you to lose your life. It can result in your imprisonment in this life and in your living in hell in future lives. One of the strongest forms of desire is sexual desire. When we enjoy the sexual embrace, we are clasping no more than a skeleton covered with flesh and skin. It has no essence other than that. The apparent beauty we find in our partner does not exist independently by itself, nor does he or she possess it right from the beginning. We are frightened by a skeleton, even though it does not move. Why then do we not fear it when it is alive and moving? Instead of being attached to such an ugly thing, why do we not pay attention to the enduring peace of nirvana?

It is not surprising that we do not recognize other bodies as filthy, but it is amazing that we do not think of our own bodies as dirty. Why is it that we prefer our bodies, with their various unpleasant secretions, to lovely fresh lotus flowers that unfold when the rays of the sun are freed from the clouds? We flinch from touching places soiled with excrement. Why then do we like to touch the bodies from which that excrement is produced? We do not like the worms and maggots that naturally grow in the dung heap, so why are we attached to bodies whose very nature is also unclean?

Not only are we unable to see our own bodies as unclean—we are also attached to the unclean bodies of others. Even attractive things like fruit and vegetables or medicinal substances, which are relatively clean, become dirty the moment we put them in our mouths. If we spit them out, we make the ground dirty. These are some of the indications that can help us understand how our bodies are unclean. If you continue to be unable to see that the body is unclean, you should visit a mortuary and examine a dead body there. Once you have experienced the fear of touching the skin of a corpse, how can you desire to touch other bodies remain the same?

The real nature of the body is that if you leave it in its natural state, its hair and nails grow horribly long. This is why we have to make a special effort to groom ourselves as if we were polishing a weapon. We are not naturally beautiful—we are ugly. And because we are ugly we try to change our shape and apply different colors to our bodies. We create an external appearance that people ignorantly find attractive. Driven by disturbing emotions like attachment, we behave in crazy ways.

Some overly ambitious people work so hard all day that they reach home totally exhausted and fall onto their beds. This is because of attachment to wealth, the reward of work. In other cases people get married but then have to go abroad to work or, as in the case of us Tibetans, leave their homeland as refugees. Being separated from their partners is a great source of suffering. They can keep in touch only by making telephone calls or writing letters. These people started out trying to do themselves some good, but separating themselves from their partners for long periods of time feels like selling themselves into servitude. You may be content with your lot, but the needs of your partner or your children disrupt your contentment. Left to yourself you might prefer a harmonious life. You might be a warmhearted person yourself, but because of your partner and children you may find it impossible to stay on good terms with your neighbors. These are some of the problems that come about in relation to the sexual desire that exists between men and women. In short, whether you are rich or poor, leading a householder's life is like a sickness.

Nowadays, there are people who suffer because they do not have children. They visit specialists and lamas in the hope of having a child. They say special prayers and take certain medications just in order to have children. For others it is the opposite. They suffer because they are about to have a child. Then they think about abortion. People who long to have children see the coming of a child as finding a treasure. But once the child has arrived and has grown into an unruly, disobedient person, the child becomes a source of anxiety. As children grow up you have to think seriously about their education. To begin with you are unable to send them to the school you choose, or you cannot decide which school is good. Finally, having struggled to get the child admitted, you find that he or she does not do well. Or he or she may successfully pass the examinations but be unable to get a good job. And even if your son or daughter finds a good job, you have to start thinking of arranging for their marriage. This is how we pass our lives. We take so much care of our children. After we have fed them and educated them, when we become old and have to lean on a stick, our eyes watery and weak, we turn to them for help. When they refuse, the only thing we can do is lament and say it would have been better not to have had such a child. Therefore, Buddha Shakyamuni himself has said that whether you are rich or poor, leading a household life is like being afflicted with disease.

It is with thoughts like these that those who become ordained as monks and nuns leave the household life. The purpose of leaving the household life is not to do business or start a new project or deceive people. The only purpose is sincere spiritual practice. If you do that and do not worry much about your food, clothing, and possessions, but engage mainly in the practice of meditation, the life of an ordained person is just wonderful. You can get up early in the morning because you do not have to depend on anyone. If you want to sleep you can sleep. On a superficial level, you do not have to get entangled with ordinary, meaningless affairs. From a broader perspective you can devote your whole life to attaining Buddhahood. In the short term you can lead a very satisfactory life if you are sincere in your practice. There is a verse that says, "If you sincerely practice, even if you stay and lead the life of a householder, nirvana will be yours. But if you do not practice, even if you remain in the mountains for years, hibernating like a marmot, you will not achieve anything."

Attachment to wealth and possessions is a source of hardship. When we have no money we can do nothing. We have to find work for the maximum pay. But you can earn good money only when you have a good education. Consequently, some people try to get a good education, while others produce fake certificates. Even simple business requires capital at the outset. Many Tibetan refugees sell sweaters and other woolen goods on the Indian streets, which can be very hard. But there are not many among them who undergo such hardship for the sake of their spiritual practice. Likewise, people perform rituals and prayers, but not many go to a lama and say, "Please perform this ritual so that I can soon attain nirvana and enlightenment." On the other hand, many people go to a lama and say, "Please perform this prayer so that I will be successful in my business." Once you have finally earned some money, there is a problem of how to protect it, which bank to put it in. Nowadays, there are so many different banks, you have to establish which will give you the greatest interest. In the meantime your earnings may be lost or stolen.

There are sensible ways to use money. I can think of one Tibetan in particular who once requested me to give a Kalachakra initiation, saying he was ready to sponsor it. After he heard me speak of the need for the education and sponsorship of children, he changed his mind and told me that he would prefer to spend the money he had earlier deposited for the initiation on the education of Tibetan children. This is exemplary and good. Having gone to the trouble to accumulate money, such people are spending it in beneficial and meaningful ways. Elsewhere I have heard of people not only offering prayers every week after someone has died, but holding a big feast to celebrate. This is very silly. How can you celebrate someone's death? When we accumulate money and make economic progress, we should ensure that it is spent positively on education, health, and so forth, not just wasted. Our human life has such great opportunities that are so difficult to find, but if we waste it in pursuit of trivial things that even animals can achieve, it is really a shame. Human life provides the basis for wonderful achievements. It would be most unfortunate to use it only to ensure the survival of this body.

When you scratch a rash you feel some kind of relief, but instead of enjoying that relief it would be better not to have a rash at all. Nobody wants to have a rash in order to have the pleasure of scratching it. Similarly, when you desire something there is some momentary pleasure to be had from obtaining it, but it would be better to have no desire or attachment at all.

When you try to focus your mind on an object, it tends to become distracted. There are two causes for the mind not being able to stay on the object. These are excitement and laxity. Initially, excitement is one of the most forceful obstructions to focusing the mind on the object. Excitement is both a distraction and a kind of attachment. The mind may be distracted either by an external object or by subtle conceptual thoughts. It must be stopped. One of the principal factors that disposes the mind to become distracted is that it gets too keyed up. When the mind is too high-spirited it becomes extremely clever. Just as we face problems when we try to be too clever, so the mind becomes too excited. When that happens it is useful to try to withdraw the mind within. To reduce the mind's high spirits, reflect on the faults of the disturbing emotions, the nature of impermanence, or the suffering nature of the cycle of existence. Reflecting on such topics is slightly discouraging, which has the effect of sobering and withdrawing the mind.

On the other hand, if the mind becomes too discouraged and loses its spirit, it will become weak and lose its power to analyze and examine. Then the mind loses its clarity and its ability to discriminate. This is mental laxity. It does not prevent the mind from abiding on its object; it prevents it from doing so with clarity. If you lose the clarity of the object, even if the mind stays on the object, you will not be able to perceive it clearly. In such circumstances you should try to invigorate the mind by reflecting on the qualities of the awakening mind, the Buddha nature that is present within you, and the fact that you have obtained a life as a free and fortunate human being. If you think in this way the mind will become fresh and clear.

With regard to the object of meditation, in general any object will do, such as a piece of stone or a flower. If you choose a flower, you should first look at it clearly. Observe its color and shape. This will generate an image of it in your mind. Whether or not the flower is within your field of vision, you should try to meditate on the mental image of it. Of the innumerable things you could select as an object of meditation, it is very useful to choose an image of the Buddha. If you do so, you will be able to accumulate great merit. You should visualize the image at a distance equivalent to a full-length prostration in front of you at the level of your brows. You should imagine that the image is luminous, but slightly heavy, to counter excitement. Seeing the image as clear and radiant counters mental laxity. This is the way to meditate as described in the sutras.

If you have received a tantric empowerment and you meditate as explained in the tantras, you visualize your body as the body of a deity and meditate on that. When you enter into the practice of Highest Yoga Tantra, you focus not simply on the whole body but on specific points within the body. There are channels visualized within the body, and when you meditate you focus on the energies flowing through them. Alternatively you can focus your attention on a particular drop within the channels. Another approach is to meditate simply on the nature of the mind, the clarity and mere luminosity of the mind. First you should stop thinking about all your past experiences, whatever you have done or has happened to you. You must also stop your mind from wandering after future plans and projects. Once you stop the arising of conceptual thoughts, the mind will be free to identify the mere luminous nature of the mind. When you have been able to do that, you should let your mind abide upon it. The mind will focus on the mind. There is a mind experiencing and a mind being experienced. This is how you use the mind as the object of your meditation.

There is also a process of cultivating the awakening mind in meditation by exchanging your own welfare for the sufferings of other sentient beings. You see yourself and other sentient beings as of equal nature. This process is very powerful. It is supported by reason and logic, but it can also be understood in the light of our own day-to-day experience.

Initially you should meditate on your equality with all other sentient beings. This means understanding that all sentient beings are like you in wanting happiness and not wanting suffering. All sentient beings not only have such a wish but also have a right to find happiness and eliminate suffering. Therefore, without partiality, without attachment, without anger you should cultivate a mind willing to benefit all sentient beings. All sentient beings also have the same potential as you to find happiness and remove suffering. These are the aspects in which they are the same as yourself. This can be understood easily by simple observation. Even the tiniest insects are like you in wanting happiness and not wanting suffering. If a tiny insect is moving toward you and you put out your finger to touch it, it will back off and stay quiet, trying to protect itself. Even though such an insect is so fragile and weak, it tries its best to remove its sufferings and to cultivate happiness. Watching such helpless insects I cannot help but feel sad.

Even the gods are the same as us in wanting happiness and not wanting suffering, as are those beings who live in the realm of spirits. We often ascribe misfortune to the harm caused by evil spirits. But instead of blaming them in this way, we should reflect that spirits too are the same as us in wanting happiness and not wanting suffering. If you can see all sentient beings as of the same nature, you will not have to invite lamas to perform rituals to subdue evil spirits. You will not have to waste your money and resources.

I was once told about a strong evil spirit near where I live in Dharamsala, and I was asked to come and deal with it. I agreed, as if I knew how to expel evil spirits, because there was nothing else to do. I went there and meditated on love and compassion and reflected strongly on the fact that all beings are of the same nature in wanting happiness and not wanting suffering. I thought specifically of how the so-called evil spirit present there also possessed the same nature. Subsequently, I was told that the evil spirit had gone or was giving no more trouble. Maybe it was just a coincidence, or maybe I achieved some success. In almost every case, meditating sincerely on compassion really helps such beings. If you compare the circumstances of the allegedly harmful spirit with those of the victim, the spirit is worse off. We at least have the opportunity to do spiritual practice, which provides even more reason for compassion.

Because all sentient beings are like ourselves, having the same nature, we should try to protect them. Your body has many parts: arms and legs and so forth. Even though each part is different, you try to protect them all because they belong to your body. There are countless sentient beings in the realms of existence. Since they are all like ourselves in wanting happiness and not wanting suffering, we should try to protect them from suffering. You might question this by saying, "My legs and hands may be different, but at least they belong to me. When my leg or hand is hurt it gives me pain. But when other sentient beings are hurt I feel no pain. Their sufferings do not hurt me, so why should I protect them from suffering?"

Of course other sentient beings' sufferings do not hurt you directly, but by thinking of them as being like yourself you will try to take care of them. Countless sentient beings are kind to you; therefore, their sufferings are like your sufferings. When you see them as pleasing, attractive, and kind to you, you feel you must try to relieve them of their suffering. Since it is sentient beings who are suffering, their pain should be removed, just as if it were your own suffering. Since you and other sentient beings are the same in wanting happiness, why do you make a distinction between yourself and them? Why are you concerned only for your own happiness? Since you and other sentient beings are the same in not wanting suffering, why do you make a distinction between yourself and them, protecting yourself alone and not others?

Now, if you compare which is the more important, you are just one individual, while others are infinite. Moreover, when you talk about yourself and other sentient beings, the two are not unrelated. Their actions influence you, and your actions affect the minds of other people.

The happiness and suffering that you experience are also experienced by other sentient beings. The two are related, but in terms of numbers, the welfare, peace, and happiness of other sentient beings are more important. It is thus natural to set aside the minor concern, your own welfare, in the interest of the greater concern, the welfare of others. It would be wise and skillful to sacrifice one finger, if by doing so you could protect the other nine. To sacrifice nine fingers in order to protect one would be stupid and foolish. Similarly, if ten people were due to be executed, but by sacrificing the life of one the others could be saved, it would be wise to do so.

You may reply that if other people's sufferings do not directly harm you, there is no need for you to protect them. However, although their sufferings may not affect you in the short term, they will harm you indirectly. In general, if others are happy, you will be happy. If you concern yourself with the peace and happiness of other sentient beings, you will automatically be peaceful and happy yourself. If you neglect the peace and happiness of other sentient beings and think only of yourself, if you take other people's lives, rob them of their wealth, or run off with their partners, you will create a great deal of suffering. Even from the legal point of view, if you take someone's life you will be caught and punished. If you save someone from drowning, you will be praised and rewarded. This is not just a spiritual matter; it is relevant to our daily life.

You might feel that you need not be concerned about the suffering of others because they are different people, and you cannot experience their suffering. Yet at the same time, as someone who believes in rebirth, you have to take steps to avert suffering in future lives, knowing that sooner of later you will have to encounter those sufferings. There is a fault in this way of thinking, because it tends to see the person you are now and the person you will be in the future as one. Of course, the continuity is the same, but they are two separate persons. The person accumulating the cause is not the same person who experiences the result. You think of these two different continuities, the continuum of your past life and the continuity of your next life, as your previous and future continuums. They are labeled as such on the basis of the collection of your physical and mental constituents. These designations are made on the basis of different collections and different continuities. Therefore, they have no intrinsic existence.

A rosary or an army is similarly false and has no intrinsic existence. When many parts such as arms and legs are assembled together we designate or call them a body. When many beads are strung together we call them a rosary. When many soldiers are gathered together we call them an army. The person who possesses suffering is also a designation and has no intrinsic existence. There is no substantially existent owner who experiences suffering. We cannot make a distinction. If we are concerned about the suffering of the other person we will be in the future, we should be concerned about the sufferings of other persons now. Ultimately everything is empty of intrinsic existence; there is no true owner of suffering. Suffering is suffering, and it must be dispelled.

Another question that might be raised here is that although we all do not want suffering, when we generate compassion, we concern ourselves with the sufferings of other sentient beings. This amounts to bringing additional suffering upon ourselves. You might ask why we should persistently cultivate such compassion. The answer to this is that when you think about the sufferings of other sentient beings, you also reflect on the reasons for helping them. You cultivate compassion voluntarily, on the basis of reason, so it does not contribute to even greater suffering. The kind of natural suffering we experience does not occur because we have taken it on voluntarily. Therefore, when such sufferings arise we get desperate and our minds are overwhelmed. On the other hand, if you voluntarily undergo hardship to be able to practice, because of your determination it will no longer be a hardship. Instead of feeling defeated in the face of such hardship, you will feel more courageous. Because you know the reason why you are facing such hardship, it will neither overpower nor discourage you. In fact, it will make you happy.

When you cultivate compassion you think about how sentient beings suffer, you think about how they are kind to you, and you think about the reasons for removing their sufferings. Consequently you are not discouraged. You might feel slightly uneasy faced with the sufferings of other sentient beings, but it will not discourage your mind. Therefore, there is a clear distinction between the overpowering suffering that comes about as a natural process of being born in the cycle of existence and the kind of hardship that you encounter voluntarily on the basis of reason and with a view to the benefit that will ensue. If by encountering hardship or suffering or by voluntarily accepting one hardship or one suffering you are able to eliminate many sufferings, it is proper to do so. Therefore, those possessing compassion find it worthwhile to cultivate such hardship within themselves. If you habituate your mind in this way, you will be very happy to remove the sufferings of other sentient beings. You will engage in such conduct just as a swan voluntarily enters a lake filled with lotuses. With this kind of attitude, even if you have to be born into hell in order to remove the suffering of sentient beings, you will do so gladly. When all beings are free, will not happiness spread far and wide like the ocean?

If you fulfill the wishes of other sentient beings, it is nothing to be especially proud of. You need not boast about it. Since your sole purpose is to help fulfill the purposes of other sentient beings, there is no ground for expecting some positive reward. Just as you guard yourself from even minor difficulties like unpleasant words, you should cultivate a mind to protect sentient beings. This is the kind of compassion you should aim for. Once your mind is familiar with it, you will come to regard others the way you do yourself.

This method of cultivating the awakening mind, which places greater emphasis on the needs of others than on your own, should be developed if you have not developed it. It should be strengthened if you have already cultivated it. You should see yourself as riddled with faults and others as possessing oceanlike qualities. This means that self-centeredness should be seen as a fault, while concern for other sentient beings is the source of oceanlike qualities. Therefore, you should engage in the practice of exchanging yourself with others. Give up self-centeredness and meditate on accepting other sentient beings.

There is no self existing intrinsically from beginningless time. Still, you have come to regard this physical entity that was produced by your parents as your body. If you let your mind become accustomed to the idea, why could you not come to regard other sentient beings in the same way? Then working for other sentient beings and undergoing difficulties on their behalf will not be something to boast about. When you feed yourself, you do not expect something in return. Therefore, just as you protect yourself even from minor disturbances like hearing unpleasant words, you should cultivate a mind to protect sentient beings. You should get used to the mind of compassion.

Even though such practices are difficult, do not let that stop you from doing them. Do not think that you cannot do it because it is difficult. Do not get discouraged and turn back. Great compassion is very beneficial and useful. Just now it may be beyond the reach of your mind, but once you get accustomed to it you will be able to generate it. For example, there may be someone who you feel is very hostile toward you. As a result, whenever you hear that person's name you feel afraid. But once you actually become acquainted with him or her, you gradually become very close. If you want to protect yourself and other sentient beings, you must engage in the secret practice of exchanging yourself with other sentient beings. Exchanging yourself with others is called the supreme secret practice and should be done with a wish to attain Buddhahood. Indeed, in order to attain Buddhahood you must exchange yourself with others. Exchanging yourself with other sentient beings is difficult for people with narrow minds or little intelligence to understand or appreciate. Therefore, it is in relation to such people that it is called a supremely secret practice.

You might think that if you give up your body and possessions, there will be nothing left for you to enjoy. If you worry like this, you are still concerned with your own interests. "If I give this, what will I use?" is the voice of self-centeredness. "If I use this, what will I have to give?" is the voice of concern for other sentient beings. That is the virtuous practice, the spiritual practice. Similarly, harming other sentient beings for your own interests, killing animals for their meat or skin, robbing others of their wealth, lustfully committing rape, deceiving people and speaking to them harshly, however you harm them physically, mentally, or verbally, will lead to an unbearably painful life in hell. On the other hand, if out of concern for others you free sentient beings, help them, and save their lives, if you voluntarily accept hardship and suffering on their behalf, you will achieve all excellent qualities. In the short term you will be born as a free and fortunate human being, and ultimately you will attain liberation and enlightenment.

If you think highly of yourself and long to occupy a superior position, you will have many enemies in this life. People will talk badly about you and you will be surrounded by hostility. In the future your senses will be dull and you will be foolish. If instead you humbly occupy a lower position, others will respect you in this life. It may sometimes seem that it is bullies who succeed. This is perhaps the way of politicians, who make so many promises and boasts during their election campaigns that they will do this or that. But it is just such reckless lies that contaminate the whole political atmosphere. If you observe humility and regard others as your superiors, you will be happy in this life and achieve peace and happiness in future lives.

Out of selfishness you may compel others to work for you. For example, people use horses and other animals to carry goods without care for their welfare. They think of them only as something to be used. Such animals regularly have sores on their backs. The result of enslaving other creatures is to be born as an enslaved creature yourself. However, if you dedicate your own body, speech, and mind as objects of enjoyment for all the infinite sentient beings, you will in the future be born into a good family and will be beloved by all.

In short, every kind of peace and happiness in this world is the result of being willing to benefit other sentient beings or of actually benefiting other sentient beings. Whatever disturbances we encounter, whatever unsatisfactory states of existence we find ourselves in, all are the results of desiring peace and happiness for ourselves alone. They are due to self-centeredness. All the excellent qualities we enjoy in the cycle of existence right up to the attainment of Budhahood are the results of concern for the welfare of others. There is no need to say more. Consider the difference between us ordinary childlike beings and the Buddha Shakyamuni. For countless lives we have thought only of our own interests and always been concerned for ourselves. Look at our plight. The Buddhas, on the other hand, have for countless lives ignored their own welfare and happiness and concerned themselves solely with the welfare of other sentient beings. The difference between us and the Buddhas is obvious.

Normally we are occupied with our own peace or suffering, and we forget about the peace and suffering of other sentient beings. Now we can change this by cultivating concern for the peace and suffering of other sentient beings and neglecting our own interests. If we do not exchange our peace and happiness for the sufferings of other sentient beings, not only will we not attain Buddhahood, but even here in the cycle of existence we will have no happiness. Because all fear, suffering, and harm arise from our misconception of an intrinsically existent self, we will not be able to eliminate suffering. If we do not let go of fire, we cannot avoid being burned.

Therefore, in order to avert harm from yourself and eliminate the sufferings of other sentient beings, you should offer yourself to other sentient beings and you should cherish other sentient beings as you would yourself. Henceforth, you should think of yourself as belonging to other sentient beings. You must make sure that your mind understands the new situation. Since you have offered yourself to other sentient beings, your sole task is to fulfill their wishes. Since you have offered them to others, you can no longer use your eyes, your body, or your speech to fulfill your own interests. You should always give the greater importance to other sentient beings. Whatever good things you possess, you should snatch up and use to benefit other sentient beings.

Ordinarily, those worse off than you are jealous, those who are equal are competitive, and those better off than you bully you. In turn you bully those worse off than you, compete with your equals, and are jealous of those better off than you. Let us visualize these three categories of people: those who are worse off, those who are equal to us, and those who are better off than us. Having cultivated some aspiration to the awakening mind, imagine taking the side of each of these three categories of people and feel jealousy, competitiveness, and a bullying attitude toward your old self. In other words, cultivate a fresh intention to side with sentient beings and denigrate your old self. Be jealous of your old self, be competitive with your old self. You might find it easier to adopt the role of a meditator, an eyewitness. On the one side imagine the group of helpless sentient beings, and on the other imagine your old self. Your old self is the self who has always been self-centered, absorbed in its own interests. It is the one that has been used to bullying the worse off, competing with equals, and feeling jealous of the better off.

When you adopt an impartial attitude toward the negative deeds of your old self, you cannot help siding with the group of sentient beings. You are able to see the faults of your old self. Siding with sentient beings who are worse off than you, feel jealousy for your old self. Siding with sentient beings equal to you, feel competitiveness with your old self, and siding with sentient beings better off than you, look down on your old self. In other words, imagine siding with these different groups of sentient beings and regarding your old self-centered self as a different person. Then you should deliberately meditate on jealousy, competitiveness, and pride.

First is the meditation on jealousy, in which you side with the helpless sentient beings worse off than you. You reflect that your old self-centered self is respected, while we, meaning all other sentient beings, are not. Your old self has many possessions and receives high praise, while we are derided and defamed. The old self-centered self has peace and happiness, while we endure only toil, suffering, and hardship. The old self is widely reputed in the world, while we are regarded as inferior and without qualities.

Sentient beings' problems, like not being able to observe morality, are not innate or natural qualities. They arise because of the power of the disturbing emotions. It is not that sentient beings are bad by nature. If the old self had any good qualities, he should use them to help and nurture sentient beings. He should be able to bear the difficulties involved. Because of the self-centered self's neglect, we sentient beings are being thrown into the mouth of unfavorable existence. The old self not only has no compassion for sentient beings but also brags and boasts of his own qualities. This is how you generate competitiveness.

Again, there is a meditation focusing on competing with your old self. In order to see sentient beings as superior to the old self, imagine that we have possessions and respect. We advertise our qualities to the world and conceal the qualities of the old self. If we hide our faults, we will be respected and given gifts, but the old self will not. If the old self-centered self does something improper, we will watch for a long time and enjoy his humiliation.

Next is a meditation on seeing sentient beings as superior. The deluded old self cannot compete with us. Even though he wants to, there is no competition, because in terms of learning, wisdom, beauty, and possessions the old self-centered self is not equal to us. When our qualities are proclaimed, we sentient beings will experience mental and physical pleasure. We will be able to enjoy peace and happiness. Although the old self has some possessions, since he is working for us, we will give him simply enough to live on and snatch away the rest. Let his good fortune decline. We shall do him harm, just as he has so long done to us.

For countless eons our self-centered attitude has brought us only harm in the cycle of existence. Each and every sentient being longs to fulfill its own ambitions. Nevertheless, they do not know how to do so. Despite undergoing incredible hardship for countless eons, they have achieved nothing but suffering. From beginingless time up to this point now you have cherished yourself. Even though you have tried your best to improve your present plight, you have failed in the pursuit of happiness. Continuing to cherish yourself will not change the present situation. This is why you should definitely start to fulfill the wishes of other sentient beings and remove their sufferings.

You should train your mind to be primarily concerned for the welfare of other sentient beings. To do so is to act in accordance with the teachings of the Buddha, which are sound and reliable. Gradually the advantages of concern for other sentient beings will emerge. Had you long ago engaged in the practice of exchanging your own welfare for the sufferings of other sentient beings, by now you could have achieved the excellent qualities of a Buddha.

Therefore, just as you have come through force of habit to regard the result of the union of your parents' sperm and ovum as "I," through familiarity you should also be able to generate a similar attitude toward other sentient beings. When you appreciate the faults of self-centeredness, you must try to destroy it and voluntarily concern yourself with the happiness of other sentient beings. Having determined to practice for the sake of other sentient beings, if you work for the sake of other sentient beings, whatever good physical qualities or belongings you may possess, steal them and put them to use to benefit other sentient beings.

At this point think of the old self-centered self as yourself once more, "You are happy and others are unhappy. You are well off and others are badly off. You look after yourself but not others. Why am I not jealous of you?" Set yourself apart from happiness and take the sufferings of other sentient beings upon yourself. From this point on, in your normal life, whether it is day or night, whether you are coming or going, sitting or sleeping, you should watch how you think. Use mindfulness and alertness to examine your faults. When you see other sentient beings behaving badly, accept their faults as your own. And if you commit even a minor mistake, declare it openly to others. When you praise the reputation of another, let it outshine your own. Put yourself at the service of others. Do not commend your faulty self just to obtain some fleeting benefit. Until now, looking after only yourself, you have always brought harm to other sentient beings. Now, pray that all such harm and suffering fall upon yourself in order to do them some good. Do not let your mind become agitated or coarse. Let it be calm and peaceful.

This is how you could think and actually behave. If the self-centered attitude does not comply, immediately and forcibly bring it under control. Under the sway of self-centeredness from time immemorial, you have brought yourself only harm and suffering. Now take control of this misplaced attitude and destroy it. If your mind does not comply, even after so much advice, the only thing you can do is to destroy your self-centered attitude. It is based on a mistake. Moreover, self-centeredness has repeatedly been the end of you in the past. When you were ignorant and confused, when you did not know how to cultivate the causes of happiness or how to eliminate the causes of suffering, self-centeredness took advantage and destroyed you.

Those days are gone and belong to the past. Now you can see how self-centeredness brings harm and destruction. If you still feel inclined to pursue your own interests, cast such misguided attitudes aside. Now that you have sold your self-interest to others, do not get discouraged. Offer your service, your capacity, and your potential to help sentient beings. If you carelessly fail to put your self-interest at the service of other sentient beings, the consequent negativity will bring you destruction and harm. If you allow it to overpower you, it will destroy you and throw you into hell. Appreciating the dire results that ensue, stop thinking about yourself alone. If you want to protect yourself, generate a mind concerned for the welfare of other sentient beings. Protect and guard them instead. The more you protect and guard your body, the more helpless it will become. It will not be able to tolerate even minor sufferings and problems. You will fall into even greater impotence. Having helplessly fallen, you will generate further attachment. And because of your attachment, even if you obtain every treasure the earth can provide, none of it will satisfy or fulfill you.

Finally, this body, which you think so much of and which you have taken such care of, will die. It will collapse. The mind leaves the body, which turns into a corpse. Then the body will be unable to move, because it is consciousness that animates it. As soon as the consciousness departs, the body begins to decay and rot. This body is only a source of fear, so why do you cherish it so much? From an objective point of view, the body is like a piece of wood. Although you sustain it with food and drink, the body does not remember your kindness. Even when it is being devoured by vultures, the body shows no displeasure. It recognizes neither the kindness nor the harm being done it, so why do you feel attached to this body? Likewise, the body is unaware whether it is praised or blamed, so why do you tire yourself out for its sake?

If you are attached to your body in the way that you are fond of an old friend, surely, since all sentient beings feel the same toward their bodies, you should have affection for the bodies of all sentient beings. Therefore, for the sake of all sentient beings, give up attachment to this body. And although it has many faults and is by nature made up of unpleasant, filthy substances, if you are able to employ it purposefully, use the body as a tool to fulfill your various aims. Until now, like a child's, your behavior has been trivial. Now is the time to change and follow the path of the wise. Like the compassionate Buddhas and bodhisattvas, you should accept what has to be done. Otherwise, how will you put an end to suffering?

CHAPTER 8

Wisdom

All the practices that were previously explained, the practices of generosity, patience, and so forth, were taught by the Buddha for the sake of the practice of wisdom. Wisdom means many things. There is, for example, the wisdom of the five sciences. Here we are dealing with the wisdom realizing emptiness, the wisdom that understands reality. The great Indian master Nagarjuna said,

> I pay homage to the Buddha
> Who taught the incomparable teaching
> That dependent arising and emptiness
> Are of the same meaning as the middle way.

A Buddha possess many physical, verbal, and mental qualities, but here the Buddha is being hailed in terms of wisdom, his precise realization that the meaning of emptiness, dependent arising, and the middle way are synonymous. There are important reasons for this. The teaching of dependent arising has vast implications. In general, everything comes into existence in dependence on other factors and conditions. For example, our experiences of happiness and suffering arise only in dependence on specific causes. Since we want happiness, we should discover its causes and implement them in practice. Since we do not want suffering, we should discover its causes and eliminate them. That is the meaning of the teaching of the Four Noble Truths.

This is what the Buddha taught during his first turning of the wheel of doctrine, when he explained the Four Noble Truths: that there is suffering, that suffering has a cause, that cessation of suffering is possible, and that there is a path to that cessation. What we actually want is happiness. The happiness we experience while we are still wandering in the cycle of existence is undoubtedly a kind of happiness, but it is not stable. What we really desire is lasting happiness. Total separation from suffering is a stable and reliable form of happiness. That is the object we wish to achieve, and what will help us achieve it is the path.

Since things arise and come into existence in accordance with their causes, the Buddhist scriptures contain no presentation of a self that experiences happiness and suffering independent of causes. Likewise, they do not assert an independent creator of the universe. Assertions of an independent self or an independent creator contradict the presentation that things arise merely in dependence on their causes. When we accept that everything is conditional, it is logical that we cannot accept a self that is permanent, partless, and independent. Likewise, it would be contradictory and logically inconsistent to accept an independent creator of the universe.

The reason used to prove that phenomena lack intrinsic existence is that they come into existence in dependence upon other causes. They also depend on their parts, and they depend on the thought that designates them with names. However, the fact that things are devoid of intrinsic existence does not imply that they do not exist at all. Things exist because of the coming together of many factors, and because they come into existence in dependence on these factors, things lack independence, things lack intrinsic existence. The point here is to demonstrate that emptiness means dependent arising. If we understand emptiness as meaning dependent arising, we will not fall into the extreme of nihilism. Likewise, when we talk about things arising in dependence on causes, we understand that they do not have independent existence, and this counters the extreme view of permanence. Therefore, it is taught that emptiness, dependent arising, and the middle way all signify the same thing.

Because all phenomena are empty of intrinsic existence, the disturbing emotions that afflict our minds are not inborn or intrinsic qualities of the mind. They are not present in the mind from the beginning. They arise as a result of negative thoughts and consequently can be removed. From the beginning, the mind has the qualities of clarity and awareness. These are primordial qualities of the mind. Attachment and hatred arise temporarily from incidental circumstances and thus can be eliminated. The possibility of removing those elements that contaminate the mind and cultivating qualities of a Buddha is an intrinsic quality of the mind.

Even among the followers of the Buddha himself there were people with diverse mental dispositions and interests. Taking this into account, he gave various levels of explanation of his teachings. This is why we find apparently different meanings in the various scriptures taught by the Buddha. Consequently, his teachings can be classified either as definitive or as requiring interpretation. By distinguishing his definitive discourses, the teachings that can be accepted literally, we can pursue the actual thought of the Buddha concerning the ultimate mode of existence of things.

An example can be found in a text called the *Treasury of Knowledge*, where the sizes of the sun and the moon are compared to half the height of Mount Meru, the mountain that is said to form the axis of the universe. The measurement is given in ancient terms and is equivalent to about four hundred miles. These scriptures are referring to the same sun and moon that scientists can measure today. What is asserted in the scriptures is at variance with direct perception using scientific instruments. We cannot defend what is stated in the text when it is contradicted by scientific knowledge. Thus, although something in the scriptures may have been taught by the Buddha, whom we regard as a valid teacher, if what is taught in the text does not stand up to reason, we cannot accept it literally. We have to interpret it in terms of the Buddha's purpose and intention in giving it.

For example, when the nature of the mind of death is explained in the *Treasury of Knowledge*, it is stated that the mind of death may be virtuous or nonvirtuous. However, another text, the *Compendium of Knowledge*, explains that the dying mind can only be a neutral. Then in the Highest Yoga Tantras it is explained that we can even perform virtuous practices at the time of death. These explanations do not agree, and it is perhaps difficult to harmonize them through reason. When we find slight differences in the way things are explained in the various texts of the sutras and tantras, we should recall that the Highest Yoga Tantra texts focus especially on the presentation of the mind. The Highest Yoga Tantras classify many levels of subtle and gross mind, and they explain how to focus specifically on them. Many of the processes of yogic practice can be proved through reason and can also be gauged to some extent through our own experience. Therefore, when we take these tantric texts as our main point of reference, what is explained in the other texts has to be subject to interpretation and cannot be accepted literally.

Nowadays, in the field of science there are many disciplines like cosmology, neurobiology, psychology, and particle physics, disciplines that are the result of generations of scientific investigation. Their findings are closely related to Buddhist teachings. Consequently, I believe it is very important for Buddhist scholars and thinkers to become better acquainted with these subjects. At the same time there are many things that scientists do not accept. There are two possible reasons for this. It may be that something is not accepted because it is found to be nonexistent. But it is also possible that it is not accepted because its existence has not yet been proven. For example, scientific investigation of the existence of a particular subject may reveal a multitude of logical fallacies. If we then persisted in accepting its existence, it would contradict reason. If it can be clearly proved that something that should be findable if it exists cannot be found under investigation, then from a Buddhist point of view we accept that it does not exist. If this somehow contradicts some aspect of Buddhist doctrine as contained in the scriptures, we have no other choice but to accept that that teaching is in need of interpretation. Thus, we cannot accept a teaching literally simply because it has been taught by the Buddha; we have to examine whether it is contradicted by reason or not. If it does not stand up to reason, we cannot accept it literally. We have to analyze such teachings to discover the intention and purpose behind them and regard them as subject to interpretation. Therefore, in Buddhism great emphasis is laid on the importance of investigation.

There can be various categories of investigation. Because it is the human mind that carries out the investigation, this mind should be unmistaken about the object it is focused on. What is determined by such a mind is reliable. However, we cannot rely on what is determined by a mistaken or doubtful mind. Therefore, a very detailed presentation of the mind needs to be made. Unlike our investigations of the external world, when we investigate the nature of the mind, our primary aim is to bring about some form of positive change. We are seeking to bring about a transformation within our minds, transforming our undisciplined and untamed state of mind into a state of calmness and serenity. This is why in Buddhist literature we find extensive discussions of the nature of the mind and mental factors. There is also detailed explanation of the changes in an individual's state of mind as he or she passes from an initial state of misconception to a state of knowledge and awareness.

When it comes to more profound aspects of the nature of the object, the process of moving from misconception to knowledge is gradual. For instance, we might start out in a state of total misconception, single-mindedly holding a view contrary to reality. As we proceed with our investigation, coming to understand the reasons that challenge our viewpoint, our mind changes from a state of total misconception to a wavering state of doubt. We begin to think that it could be this way or that way. Further investigation leads us on from that wavering state of mind to seeing that our previous conviction was wrong. This is the state of correct assumption. However, at this point we may still not have ascertained the object as it is apprehended by a valid mind. Gradually we will come to have a valid mind capable of drawing the correct conclusion. When we then meditate on the meaning we have understood, we will develop familiarity with it. Eventually, when we achieve clarity concerning the topic of meditation, the mind will become a direct and valid consciousness. This is how the mind is trained.

When the mind is undertaking such an investigation, one aspect of the process is first to know that things have a natural and innate mode of existence. Because of this, when the mind enters into investigation, it searches for truth or reality. Reality is not something that the mind has fabricated anew. Therefore, when we search for the meaning of truth, we are searching for reality, for the way things actually exist. Whether we are dealing with external or internal phenomena, it is important to understand their mode of existence and how they function. This is called the logic of suchness, which means that we investigate things on the basis of their suchness or nature. In the case of the mind, for example, we need first to recognize its natural processes. We need to be able to distinguish between the mere clarity of the mind and those aspects that appear when extraneous factors such as attachment arise.

Another type of investigation is, for example, to examine our experience in the course of one day. If we feel unhappy in the morning it can color other feelings throughout the day, even though there may not be a direct causal relationship between our earlier feeling of unhappiness and our subsequent feelings. It happens because of the influence of a particular thought on our mental state. In the case of physical materials as well, two different substances can come together to produce a substance possessing altogether different qualities from either of them individually. We can observe this in chemical reactions. In the case of our minds, if we experience a strong thought in the morning we may feel slightly happier or unhappier during the day because of the imprints left by that thought. Because of a feeling of unhappiness we may be more easily provoked. Little things may make us angry. On the other hand, it may be that because of a strong feeling of happiness one day, even when someone makes a mistake, we treat it lightly and put up with it. Clearly the changes in our minds are dependent on the coming together of many diverse situations and circumstances. Encountering happy circumstances disposes us to take disturbances or misfortunes lightly, whereas upsetting circumstances leave us intolerant and easily provoked.

It is true that there is no phenomenon that is not designated by the mind. But this does not mean that whatever is designated by the mind must necessarily exist. For example, we could imagine a rabbit's horn, but in reality no rabbit has a horn. If whatever is designated by the mind must necessarily exist, then the horn of the rabbit should also exist. Therefore, it is true to say that although there is no phenomenon that is not designated by thought, that does not mean that whatever is designated by thought necessarily exists. We need to know the way things exist. Since the laws of nature cannot be changed at will by thought, we have to accept them as they are and follow a process of transforming the mind that does not contradict them. This is how we will be able to cultivate happiness and minimize suffering.

Because we feel unhappy as a result of anger, we say it would be good if we could eliminate anger. Because we feel happy as a result of compassion and loving-kindness, we say it is good to develop these qualities. Now, anger and loving-kindness are to some extent opposed to each other, if not mutually exclusive. Therefore, we reason that, since these two minds possess opposing characteristics, if we make an effort to cultivate and develop loving-kindness, our anger will be weakened. This is how we can pursue our spiritual endeavor. We make efforts to cultivate loving-kindness and dispel anger, because anger is a cause of unhappiness and loving-kindness is a cause of happiness.

It is important to investigate things in this way. We are seeking the meaning of the truth and we can gain conviction regarding the truth through analysis and investigation. The great Indian commentator Haribhadra described two categories of people who follow the Buddha's teachings. There are those with sharp intelligence who follow the teachings through reason and those with less intelligence who follow the teachings by relying on faith. Those with sharp intelligence examine the meaning of the teachings. They use reason to investigate whether the teachings contain any logical fallacies. When they have largely satisfied themselves that the teachings are free from logical inconsistencies and have a valid foundation, they feel confident and inspired to follow them, even though they might not yet have thoroughly fathomed their meaning. The general method presented in these teachings for eliminating the faults of the mind relies on the use of reason. Someone who has doubts about a particular topic is also a good candidate for the use of reason. This is why I often tell people that if they wish to become Buddhist practitioners they should first be skeptical.

In our lives, we engage in countless activities and receive huge sensory input from the world around us. We tend to see all these activities and the phenomena that appear to us as absolutely true. In other words, we are deceived into thinking that things exist in the way they appear to us. This discrepancy between how things appear and how they really exist is the source of much of our trouble. Consequently, examining this discrepancy and investigating reality, the ultimate mode of existence, is the nexus of all Buddhist philosophical thought. The ultimate mode of existence is established through analysis, investigation, and experiment.

All Buddhist schools of thought accept what are known as the four seals: all composite things are impermanent, all contaminated things are miserable, all phenomena are empty and selfless, and nirvana is peace. All conditioned phenomena, right from the time they come into existence, are fleeting by nature and do not stay even for an instant. This momentariness is a result of the cause itself; no other factor is involved. Everything that is composed of parts, or conditioned by causes and conditions, is impermanent and fleeting. These things do not stay forever; they continually disintegrate. This kind of subtle impermanence is confirmed by scientific findings.

Impermanent, composite phenomena are, in general, the results of causes. We are particularly concerned here with the nature of our collection of physical and mental components that make up the person. These are the results of disturbing emotions and misguided or contaminated actions, which is why they are referred to as contaminated objects. The disturbing emotions are dominated by ignorance, the misconception of intrinsic existence. To be subject to ignorance and the other disturbing emotions is suffering, and freedom from them is peace. This is what is meant by saying all contaminated things are miserable.

The question we have to address is whether we have to undergo suffering endlessly. The third statement, all phenomena are empty and selfless, makes clear that we do not. In reality all phenomena are empty and selfless. That is their actual state. Even though that is their real state, things appear to have intrinsic existence. This perception of things being intrinsically existent is a wrong consciousness, a mistaken way of thinking. It has no valid foundation. We have such a strong misconception, not on the basis of valid reasons or some other solid foundation, but because of long habituation to error. If we now make an effort to understand the meaning of emptiness and the nature of selflessness, we will be able to remove our misconceptions and gain an insight into the true nature of things. The cause of our misconceptions, disturbing emotions, can be removed. Our ignorance, the misconception of intrinsic existence, can be eliminated. Once we remove these contaminated causes, we will attain a state of peace. Therefore, nirvana is peace. Nirvana is called peace because it is undeceptive and reliable.

The foundation of all Buddhist teaching and practice is the principle of dependent arising. Why is this? First of all, practices related to establishing ultimate truth, an understanding of the emptiness of true existence, are possible only because of dependent arising. Since things arise in dependence on other causes and conditions, they are naturally free from independent and autonomous existence. By using such reasons, we refute our misconceptions about intrinsic existence. Therefore, it is through understanding the meaning of dependent arising that we can develop a fresh understanding of the view of emptiness and develop and promote it further. Second, since things arise in dependence on other factors, we can understand that our own happiness and suffering are the results of our own actions. Similarly, the majority of our positive and negative experiences involve other sentient beings. If we neglect them, we lose, and if we take care of them, we too will benefit. These instructions are based on the principle of dependent arising. Thus, the whole Buddhist way of life is derived from the notion of dependent arising. The Buddhist conduct of non violence, seeking not to harm others, its view of selflessness, and the meditation practices related to them all rest on the foundation of dependent arising.

Emptiness is another way of explaining dependent arising. And by using the reasoning of dependent arising, you will be able to understand that things lack intrinsic existence, are empty of intrinsic existence. It is from the perspective that conventional phenomena are dependent and exist as designations that the undeviating relationship of cause and effect is presented. And it is in this context that we engage in such practices as compassion, love, and kindness, the practices of giving, ethics, patience, effort, and meditation.

Different categories of mind, like attachment and hatred, are based on the mind's misconception of things as having objective existence. When we cultivate a mind focused on selflessness, it opposes the misconception of true existence and thus automatically weakens the force of our attachment and hatred. Positive categories of mind, such as love and compassion, do not need the support of ignorance, the misconception of true existence, in order to grow. Indeed, when we combine the practice of emptiness and the skillful means of the awakening mind, they support each other, increasing and strengthening our mental potential. Gradually, the state of mind that understands emptiness through a mental image becomes nondualistic and transforms into the nonconceptual and direct vision of emptiness. As we become increasingly familiar with this stream of practice, all our temporary faults cease in the sphere of natural purity and the appearance of all elaborations ceases. That ultimate state of thorough pacification possessing the characteristics of total cessation of all elaborations is called the Buddha's Truth Body.

In order to overcome the disturbing emotions, you must develop the view of emptiness. As long as you misconceive your mental and physical constituents as having intrinsic existence, you will similarly misconceive the self. And when you are subject to the misconception of self, you will accumulate negative karma, and from karma arises rebirth. Therefore, in order to attain nirvana and gain liberation from the cycle of existence, it is necessary to cultivate the view of emptiness. The wisdom realizing emptiness is necessary even for those intent on personal liberation. Therefore, we should cultivate the wisdom understanding emptiness on the basis of having cultivated a calmly abiding mind. Of the various kinds of wisdom, you should cultivate specifically the wisdom that functions as an antidote to the obstructions to enlightenment. Such a wisdom should be influenced by the practice of the first five perfections. Therefore, it is said that these practices were taught in order to cultivate Buddhahood. All the teachings of the Buddha are based on the teaching of dependent arising, and they were given for the sake of departing from the state of suffering.

It is not enough simply to realize emptiness; you must become thoroughly familiar with it. You have to think about the meaning of emptiness, and you have to observe phenomena under the influence of such a mind. For example, when we observe a group of people, it is true that we all want happiness and do not want suffering. But the countless different expressions on the faces of the people are all dependent on causes and conditions. Everything is dependent on causes and conditions. Nothing has intrinsic existence. Yet even though things have no intrinsic existence, they appear as if they do. Therefore, there is a discrepancy between how things appear and how they really exist.

When you reach such an understanding, you will be able to see everything as a dream or an illusion. Once you see things in that way, you will appreciate the essencelessness of everything, and that will enable you to reduce your attachment and anger. Since all phenomena are by nature empty of inherent existence, there is nothing to gain and nothing to lose. The Seventh Dalai Lama, explaining the view of reality, says that different phenomena—forms, sounds, and so forth—appear to the six senses. He says that although there is much to see in these appearances, although they seem to be beautiful and diverse, their real mode of existence is not the way they appear. Whatever appears to your mind appears to have intrinsic existence. This is because our minds are obscured by ignorance. We should be able to understand this and as a result understand that whatever appears to our minds is due to the power of ignorance and its imprints. As soon as such appearances come to the mind, we will know that they do not exist as they appear and we will not be deceived by them.

Whether you are faced with suffering or with peace, ultimately what is there to be enjoyed and what is there to be discouraged about? To whom should you get attached and why should you get attached to them? We have our protectors, the objects of refuge, people to look down on, friends to be attached to, enemies with whom to get angry. We should see all of them as a dream, as an illusion, and maintain an equal mental attitude toward them. This does not mean that there is no distinction between good and bad or that things do not exist at all. Although desire is often described as negative, to long for nirvana is a kind of desire. On a conventional level nirvana is something to be attained, and the cycle of existence is something to be abandoned. This is why we meditate on emptiness. Therefore, it is not good to see either the cycle of existence or nirvana as having true or intrinsic existence. We have friends and enemies. People who really do harm are called enemies and people who really do benefit are called friends. There is nothing wrong with calling a friend a friend or an enemy an enemy. But it is wrong to use the reason that someone is your friend as an excuse for attachment. Likewise, it is a mistake to get angry with someone you regard as your enemy, because you think of your enemies as completely bad. That kind of attitude is wrong. On the basis of the fact that things exist as mere designations, you should be able to see everything as an illusion, as a dream.

We want happiness for ourselves, yet we see ourselves as having intrinsic existence. This kind of misconception further strengthens our self-centered attitude. When we meditate on the lama, we try to visualize him in the centre of the eight-petaled lotus at the heart. This is quite difficult to do. However, the self-centered attitude and the misconception of an intrinsically existent self rest peacefully there without effort. We continue to take refuge in and bow down to our own self-centeredness, as if it were a holy lama, and we willingly let it reside within our hearts. Look at our plight, our condition, the situation we find ourselves in as a result. The Buddhas saw the self-centered attitude as the most hostile enemy. They fought with it and became enlightened. Some of the Kadampa masters would say, "Even if my whole being is crushed under the force of disturbing emotions, I will try to bite them with my teeth and tear them apart." They would challenge the self-centered attitude: "Now that I can see that it is you, self-centeredness, who has brought me so much trouble, I will fight you and break your neck!"

This self-centeredness together with the misconception of an intrinsically existent self have always brought us suffering. This is why, despite our wanting happiness, we always face trouble, unhappiness, and suffering. This has been our plight from beginningless time. Sometimes we may have taken birth in a celestial realm. We might even have been born as king of the gods, but even at that level of existence, self centeredness and the misconception of self as intrinsically existent still rested peacefully within our minds. Therefore, we had no lasting happiness. While we remain within the cycle of existence, there is no lasting peace or happiness because of self-centeredness and the misconception of self.

Because of self-centeredness we spin again and again within the cycle of existence. Even though we repeatedly enjoy temporary peace and happiness, we get distracted, we enter into wrong paths, we fall into unfavorable states of existence, and we encounter ceaseless sufferings. Those of us who claim to be ordained followers of the Buddha may regard ourselves as good practitioners. But if in reality you are under the sway of the self-centered attitude and the misconception of self, you may think of yourself as very special and pretend to protect and give refuge to other people. Because of such pride you will fall into an unfavorable state of existence.

The way to overcome suffering is to observe the phenomena as having no intrinsic existence, to understand and meditate on that. If you regard that view with great respect you will accumulate merit, achieve liberation from the cycle of existence, and finally attain enlightenment. First you must listen to a teacher's instructions. You must study and meditate. Try to understand the essential points of practice. See all these teachings as good instructions and good advice. Mere knowledge is of no use, so you must actually practice with persistence. You might say you are doing a retreat, but inside your small room you might simply relax and remain comfortable. This is not persistence, which means sincere and serious practice. Similarly, I have heard of meditators who maintain their physical posture beautifully and can meditate for a long time. But they have little warm feeling toward their students. Their minds are always in a kind of neutral state and not much concerned about either the suffering or the happiness of other sentient beings. This is perhaps the result of always meditating in a state of mental laxity. When they meditate, such people may have let their minds become so lax that they have no clarity or feeling. Otherwise they may have been meditating on nothingness, not emptiness of intrinsic existence, but the total nonexistence of everything. Perhaps because of that they do not have much feeling.

If our practice results in our becoming a person with no heart, who shows no concern for others' peace and suffering, it is not a good practice. Therefore, not only during meditation, but also during postmeditative periods, you should always guard the doors of the senses with mindfulness, conscientiousness, and alertness. Always watch your mind. If you are meditating on the awakening mind in particular, you should always proclaim and praise the qualities of other people and hide your own qualities. Cultivate strong faith and observe the ten wholesome actions. Avoid wrong livelihood, avoid all kinds of commotion, study and meditate on the meaning of the scriptures, and work for the welfare of all beings in the universe. Let me conclude with a very powerful prayer by Shantideva, a prayer that I recite every day:

> For as long as space endures
> And for as long as sentient beings remain,
> May I also abide
> To relieve the sufferings of living beings.